Biocultural Adaptation
in Prehistoric America

Biocultural Adaptation in Prehistoric America

ROBERT L. BLAKELY, EDITOR

Southern Anthropological Society Proceedings, No. 11
Gwen Kennedy Neville, Series Editor

The University of Georgia Press
Athens 30602

Southern Anthropological Society

Founded 1966

Library of Congress Cataloging in Publication Data

Biocultural adaptation in prehistoric America.
    (Southern Anthropological Society proceedings;
no. 11)
    Papers presented at a symposium held during the
11th annual meeting of the Southern Anthropological
Society in Atlanta.
    1. Indians—Antiquities—Congresses. 2. America—
Antiquities—Congresses. 3. Archaeology—
Methodology—Congresses. I. Blakely, Robert L.
II. Title: Southern Anthropological Society.
III. Series: Southern Anthropological Society.
Proceedings: no. 11.
GN2.S9243 no. 11 [E61]   301.2   76-56343
                ISBN 0-8203-0417-4

Contents

Cover

Upper right: this woodcut, made from a drawing by Du Pratz, depicts the Natchez mortuary ceremony surrounding the death of a chieftain, Tattooed Serpent. The chief's corpse was carried from his house on his deathbed and transferred to a litter. The litter-bearers, walking in a sequence of intersecting circles, bore Tattooed Serpent to the temple for interment later. Immediately after the deceased had been placed in the temple, eight people appointed to be sacrificed were lined up in two rows in front of the temple and strangled to death by their own relatives. The chieftain's two wives also were sacrificed so that they might join Tattooed Serpent "in the country of the spirits." The three were buried in a single grave within the temple. The other eight victims were interred elsewhere. Thereafter, the chief's house was burned. (Woodcut from Du Pratz, 1758, Vol. 3, opp. p. 55.)

Lower left: this recently excavated structure from the Pine Creek site in Fulton County, Georgia, probably was used as a charnel house by prehistoric Mississippian Indians, circa A.D. 1500. Dug into the floor of the 10×16 feet structure were the separate graves of two individuals. Their remains indicated that both had been flexed and placed on their left sides with their heads pointing northeast. (Photograph courtesy of Roy S. Dickens, Jr.)

Preface

THE papers in this volume represent an attempt by anthropologists from biological and from archeological approaches to combine their contributions and insights in viewing the overall processes of biocultural adaptation. The contributors originally presented their papers in a symposium during the 11th annual meeting of the Southern Anthropological Society in Atlanta, Georgia, in April, 1976. While they do not always agree, the participants converge in their genuine interest in applying multiple perspectives and in their commitment to the creative sharing of knowledge. They are addressing the perennial questions of the nature of culture and its complex connections to human biology, and in the search for answers they are not afraid to look beyond their own disciplinary boundaries into the promising territory of the holistic study of human beings.

Special thanks for assembling this collection of scholars goes to Bob Blakely. In addition, a note of thanks is due to Bob Buffington and Martyn Hitchcock of the University of Georgia Press for their efforts in insuring a text and layout that has enabled the authors to present their data graphically. I am also grateful to Irma Honigmann for her generous advice and words of wisdom in the launching of this new series of SAS Proceedings.

Gwen Kennedy Neville
SAS Editor

Introduction: Changing Strategies for the Biological Anthropologist[1]

R OBERT L. B LAKELY

A NTHROPOLOGISTS study human behavior, past and present, through the observation of evolutionary morphology and changing patterns of learned behavior. Too often, however, anthropologists dichotomize human biology and culture, treating each as if it were an independent variable shaping and being shaped by the human experience. The contributors to this volume, mostly biological anthropologists, believe this dichotomy to be artificial and its use counterproductive to meaningful anthropological inquiry. Humans survive not through cultural adaptation nor through biological adaptation, but through *biocultural* adaptation. The most appropriate treatment of the study of humans is, therefore, a biocultural approach. The authors apply this conceptual framework to achieve a clearer understanding of prehistoric American behavior patterns. Biocultural adaptation in prehistoric America is the dynamic expression of the lives of Americans before Columbus. These studies of biocultural adaptation, moreover, are an exhortation to *all* anthropologists to combine their efforts in order to provide a more meaningful picture of all peoples.

This aim is easily articulated, but it is difficult to actualize. A few years ago, a human biologist told me that the biological anthropologist had neither the right nor the reason to tell the archeologist how to run his or her business. It was good advice. By and large, biological anthropologists do not possess the expertise, either methodologically or theoretically, to conduct the business of archeology. We do a disservice, however, to both subdisciplines and to anthropology as a whole if we bury our heads in the proverbial sands of our specialties. If we agree that one of the hallmarks and major strengths of anthropology is its holistic nature, then we are obligated to demonstrate how our specialized knowledge contributes to that of the larger discipline.

Many paleoanthropologists may have in the past deceived themselves into thinking that they were part of conjunctive, bioarcheological investigations by providing descriptive addenda to site reports. This deception was, of course, but one symptom of a common malaise revealed also in the traditional monograph, through which most anthropologists appeared as technicians, or data bearers. The osteologist/anthropologists were, in fact, until recently preoccupied with counting skeletons, assigning age and sex, measuring, and listing pathologies, primarily with an eye toward constructing racial typologies and evolutionary trends. At the same time, archeologists were principally concerned with constructing ceramic and lithic typologies and culture periods not necessarily related to bioanthropological questions. Thus the goals of the biological anthropologist and archeologist were in the past quite different and as a result were unsuited for conjunctive research designs.

Today, however, while the procedural tools of the biological anthropologist often remain the same as before, they are being put to new uses. Our *objectives* are changing. Following the interdisciplinary orientations of Laughlin (1968), Chapple (1970), Buikstra (1972), Stewart (1973), Peebles (1974), and others, both biological anthropologists and archeologists are beginning to reframe goals in order to contribute to a more holistic picture of human cultures.

In order to do this, though, it was necessary first for biological anthropologists to get our own house in order. Although we remain an untidy bunch, the reordering began over twenty years ago. In an article designed to stimulate as much as to delineate the "new physical anthropology," Washburn (1952) began the work. He argued that understanding processes should replace descriptive enumeration, that population dynamics should supplant typology, and that anthropometry should be but one of many techniques employed to answer specific questions rather than being an end in itself. The "old physical anthropology" continues to serve as a foundation for the "new," and today the new has access to sophisticated methodological devices that Washburn could not envision a quarter of a century ago.

More important than the increased sophistication of our tools, however, is an increased awareness of the integrated ecological, cultural, and biological systems that contribute to human behavior. It should be pointed out that this recognition in itself is not new to anthropology. Chapple and Coon in 1942 first introduced to the anthropological community the concept of behavioral anthropology and the attendant necessity for a systems approach. It is the widespread acceptance of this cross-disciplinary framework among students of prehistoric human biology that is new. This new orientation is undoubtedly the result of many related and unrelated events. These include the invitation for joint endeavors extended to biological anthropologists by advocates of the "new archeology." In addition, they include the advent of advanced analytical techniques—for example, multivariate statistics, the identification of genetic markers on bones, and trace element analysis—that have vastly expanded the resources available for interpretation.

This volume brings together the contributions of biological anthropologists who employ these new perspectives, new objectives, and new methodologies. All of the authors utilize skeletal biology and/or mortuary site archeology to help answer questions concerning cultural history. Our goals are three-fold: (1) to document specific ways in which biological anthropologists can contribute to studies of cultural processes, (2) to illustrate the interrelationships between the biological, cultural, and environmental variables that affect the adaptedness or maladaptedness of prehistoric populations, and (3) to demonstrate the need for cooperation among biological anthropologists, archeologists, ethnologists, and other expert investigators toward problem-solving in behavioral anthropology.

The question that must be asked at the outset is this: what can biological anthropologists add to the understanding of cultural processes? A corollary question concerns the value of data collected from cemeteries as indicators of biocultural dynamics. Obviously it is not enough for the student of culture to study mortuary sites alone. Limiting research in that way would obviate the need to excavate habitation sites and others —a direct contradiction of the principles and objectives of the holistic approach to contextual archeology. Under certain circumstances, however, cemeteries can provide data not obtainable from any other kind of site. Habitation sites reveal information on demography, population movement, nutritional standards, and social organization. The data contained in cemeteries permit us not only to contribute further to these studies, but also to explore other paradigms of human behavior. Information such as the genetic affinities of skeletal populations (Blakely 1976), microevolutionary changes (Perzigian 1975), disease vectors (Angel 1969), familial relationships (Robbins 1975), socioeconomic status (Peebles 1974), and in-group genetic systems (Kellock and Parson 1970) can best be derived from the study of skeletal series and mortuary programs.

Due to the increased awareness of the expressions of biological variation, and with the analytic treatments possible today, biological anthropologists now are able to formulate deductively testable models of biocultural interaction and behavioral patterning. It is important to caution others and ourselves, however, that while we provide a viable approach, we offer no methodological or interpretative panaceas. As do all involved investigators, the biological anthropologist becomes completely enmeshed in his or her models and methods. The scrutinizing eye of archeological documentation should serve as the steadying mechanism here and the larger perspective of anthropological biology should be the guiding force. Therein lies the collective strength of the synthetic approach to anthropological inquiry.

In fairness to the authors and the reader, I should point out that there are areas in which the contributors to this volume may not be particularly united. The first of these is geographic zone concentration. While the geographic limits of the studies presented here are pan-eastern United States, they range from Arkansas on the southwest to South Dakota on the northwest, from the Central and Lower Illinois River valleys in the Midwest to coastal Georgia in the Southeast. The second diversity is indicated by the lack of temporal constraints. Periods represented in these studies include the Archaic, Middle and Late Woodland, Mississippian, and Historic.

An additional expression of the wide variation is in the methodologies represented here. There is currently some controversy, for example, over the relative merits of osteometric data versus discrete nonmetric traits as markers of intra- and interpopulational relationships (Corruccini 1974). Both kinds of data are employed by authors in this volume. This is not the proper forum for an extended discussion of the reliability and validity of these sets of data. Suffice it to say that both types of information provide certain parameters of population variation, contingent upon the objectives of the investigator. Finally, there are differences among contributors concerning the applicability of multivariate and univariate techniques (Kowalski 1972). These arguments should not cause undue consternation. While these are important procedural considerations, the thrust of this volume is not toward procedural problems, but toward the application of these various approaches to the answering of questions about culture.

The conceptual framework that does unite us—the biocultural perspective—is well illustrated by the first article. With the advantage of hindsight, Louise Robbins argues that past attempts by American paleoanthropologists to define "types" were unproductive, not only because typologies often were misleading, but also because this preoccupation prevented researchers from recognizing the potential values of studies of microevolution, behavioral patterns, and environmental determinants. She goes on to point out that skeletons are products of both genetics *and* extrabiological variables, and while the former relationship is extensively and intensively reported in the literature, the latter is not. She suggests, then, that since the people embodied in the skeletons lived and died in a biocultural world, the only realistic approach to their study is a biocultural one. Using data from Archaic and Late Woodland skeletal series from Kentucky and Ohio, Robbins contrasts two approaches, which she regards to be the wrong and the right approaches to bioarcheological research. She concludes among other things that, contrary to contemporary thought, maize agriculture may have been maladaptive for some prehistoric populations. In addition she concludes that, through rigorous excavation techniques and new biological analyses, it has been possible to document incidences of infanticide and intentional abortion among Late Woodland peoples in Ohio. Robbins emphasizes that these phenomena of human behavior would not have been apparent if traditional archeological and biological anthropological techniques had been employed.

In his article, David Wolf tackles a question often asked and answered by archeologists. It is the following: was the emergence of the Mississippian "culture" a product of population movement, the diffusion of ideas without migration, a widespread indigenous development, or some combination of these processes? He partially attempts to resolve this issue by comparing skeletal series from six Mississippian sites in Arkansas, Illinois, and Georgia. If the populations prove to be biologically dissimilar, he maintains, this finding would negate the migration theory of Mississippian origins and support the idea of indigenous, Woodland development and/or reception of a new cultural tradition. The underlying assumption behind his research design is that there is a correlation, either positive or negative, between breeding populations and cultural systems. The existence of such a correlation is hotly debated (Downs and Bleibtreu 1972). I am inclined to agree with Wolf that there is, and was, not only a correlation but also a causal relationship between biology and culture (Blakely 1976). Implicit in his assumption is another supposition: that observed biological diversity between Mississippians ultimately reflects biological variation between Woodland groups. Wolf's article is made more interesting by the fact that he employs both metric and nonmetric variables in his analyses and concludes that both sets of data support his hypothesis. He also includes dendrographs similar to those popularized by Howells (1973) to illustrate morphometric differences but not phylogenetic relationships (Jolly and Plog 1976) between skeletal samples.

Robert Blakely in the third article uses demographic data from skeletons recovered at Etowah, Georgia, in order to partially reconstruct the health environment of the mature Mississippian culture in northern Georgia. He then suggests, on the basis of new demographic information, that social structure at Etowah appears to have combined elements of chiefdom and egalitarian societies. He argues that by adopting more than one social system, the Etowah people could have made their society more flexible and, thereby, more adaptive. Blakely is concerned that our models of social organization, while of value as measures by which we test our data, can get in the way of interpretations if we rely too heavily on them because they blind us to the inevitable exceptions to our anthropological rules.

Jane Buikstra, agreeing with Robbins, contends in the next article that human behavior can only be understood in a holistic context. This requires both intra- and interdisciplinary cooperation, an approach for which she has coined the term "bio-archeology." She brings this approach to the interpretation of behavior patterns as revealed by mortuary programs of Middle and Late Woodland peoples in the Lower Illinois River Valley. Buikstra's question is the following: what social and demographic factors contributed to the transition from Middle to Late Woodland? Her answer is complex, and that in itself is revealing. It recognizes the fact that cultural transitions are not usually as simplistic as we tend to view them (for example, culture fatigue, migration, diffusion, and the like). Buikstra develops from her work an innovative model for the interpretation of prehistoric culture change, a model that should serve as a useful tool for biological anthropologists and archeologists for years to come.

In his article, Robert Gilbert outlines the attractive prospects for the use of trace element research in archeological inquiry. In the same manner as radioactive dating techniques and soil resistivity tests, trace element analysis is an example of scientific technology that was not developed specifically for archeology but that has important archeological applications. The use of trace element research, although not strictly an example of interdisciplinary cooperation, should thus serve as yet another indication of the potential value (at least for archeologists and biological anthropologists) of a purposeful marriage between the physical sciences and anthropology. Gilbert demonstrates how trace element analysis can contribute to studies of dietary stress, disease states, growth and development of individuals, sex differences, age statuses, social class distinctions, and subsistence economy. Traditional archeological research frequently addresses these questions, but trace elements add a new dimension to these studies. As Gilbert points out, at many archeological sites, ethnozoological and ethnobotanical evidence does not permit the reconstruction of diets, a gap in knowledge that necessitates trace element research when human bones are available.

Anthony Perzigian illustrates in his article the importance of odontological studies toward the reconstruction of biological and extrabiological elements of prehistoric American life. He points out that teeth, because they do not grow once they have erupted, permanently record developmental irregularities and environmental influences throughout the lifetimes of individuals. By relating dental morphology to archeological findings from Archaic, Late Mississippian, and Protohistoric skeletal series, Perzigian is able to conclusively identify maladaptive and adaptive aspects of different subsistence patterns in the eastern United States.

In the penultimate article, Christopher Peebles evaluates from the perspective of an archeologist the contributions made by the preceding papers to his subdiscipline. Like his colleagues in biological anthropology, he argues for greater cooperation and communication between those who, although necessarily specialists, are nonetheless committed to a better understanding of human behavior. He recognizes that because our studies are diachronic, we must deal with a changing world. Since change among living organisms entails series of episodic biological and/or "cultural" responses, Peebles contends that an appropriate approach to the study of human change is through an ecological model that reflects the dynamic interaction of adapting systems. This, he says, is the direction offered by most of the authors (and especially by Robbins, Buikstra, and Perzigian). And while Peebles is occasionally critical of the authors' remarks and interpretations, he seems to be generally satisfied with the bioarcheological approach of the contributors and the information thus generated. His positive assessment should spur continued pursuit by biological anthropologists in their quest for a fuller appreciation of prehistoric human adaptation.

Eliot Chapple, in the final article, examines the papers from the viewpoint of an "anthropological biologist" (an appellation about which he is adamant and in his paper he explains why). Chapple, like Peebles, advocates a systemic approach to biological studies, but he warns biological anthropologists that prehistorians' limited access to many of the variables affecting biosocial adaptation often renders their interpretations tenuous. He is concerned in addition because biological anthropologists make certain assumptions at the outset that may not be fully justified—for instance, presupposition of a Gaussian (normal or bell-shaped) distribution prior to statistical analyses, imposition of "irrelevant" demographic theory, and presumptions concerning the extrapolation of genetic properties from skeletal material. Mathematics, statistics, genetics, and osteology do mix, of course, but Chapple's cautionary note is well taken; indeed, the old adage that "statistics can prove anything" applies to anthropology. On the other hand, biological anthropologists are aware of certain of our assumptions and sometimes fantasmagorically wish that our limited data (for example, underrepresented material culture and skeletal material, "gaps" that separate past from present behavior, and so on) did not impose assumptions upon us. This is, however, the predicament of retrodictive paleoanthropologists. Chapple nevertheless does us a valuable service with his reminder to be careful and critical of our methodologies and interpretations. Only when we are cognizant of both our strengths and weaknesses can we be prepared to honestly address the mechanisms of biocultural adaptation.

All of the authors are in accordance concerning the nature of anthropology and the role of the anthropologist. Human adaptation takes place within the interface of biology, culture, and the natural environment. This means that no aspect of the study of humans can be completely divorced from any other aspect. Therefore, the ultimate objective of anthropologists—biological as well as archeological and ethnological—is the same. That goal is to secure the fullest possible understanding of the behavior patterns of all humans, past and present. Given this objective, it behooves anthropologists to work together in order to provide meaningful statements about our biocultural processes and heritage. The biological and archeological anthropologists contributing to this volume have tried to do that for a part of the biocultural world of prehistoric Americans.

NOTES

1. It would be an impossible task to acknowledge all of the people who contributed to this volume, but not to cite some would be equally impossible. First, although obvious, I would like to thank the scholars who participated in the 1976 symposium. Their dedication to conscientious research and the dissemination of ideas made this book possible. The constructive comments of symposium discussants Peebles and Chapple were considered so important that their remarks have been included. My gratitude is also extended to the laborers of tedium, notably Karen Haley, Rebecca Holley, and Nancie Rogers, who assisted me in the daily routine of handling the paper work. Special appreciation is owed Gwen Kennedy Neville, SAS Editor, for the patience and diligence that she displayed in readying the volume for publication. Part of the expense for putting together this book was provided by the National Science Foundation, grant SOC–7503833.

REFERENCES

Angel, J. L., 1969. Paleodemography and Evolution. *American Journal of Physical Anthropology* 31:343–353.

Blakely, R. L., 1976. Biological Distance between Late Woodland and Middle Mississippian Inhabitants of the Central Illinois River Valley. In *Approaches to the Study of Prehistory: A Bio-archaeological Perspective,*

J. E. Buikstra, ed. (Evanston: Northwestern University Archaeological Program), in press.

Buikstra, J. E., 1972. *Hopewell in the Lower Illinois River Valley: A Regional Approach to the Study of Biological Variability and Mortuary Activity* (Ph.D. diss., University of Chicago).

Chapple, E. D., 1970. *Culture and Biological Man: Explorations in Behavioral Anthropology* (New York: Holt, Rinehart, and Winston).

Chapple, E. D., and C. S. Coon, 1942. *Principles of Anthropology* (New York: Holt, Rinehart, and Winston).

Corruccini, R. S., 1974. An Examination of the Meaning of Cranial Discrete Traits for Human Skeletal Biological Studies. *American Journal of Physical Anthropology* 40:425–446.

Downs, J. F., and H. K. Bleibtreu, 1972. *Human Variation: An Introduction to Physical Anthropology* (Beverly Hills: Glencoe Press).

Howells, W. W., 1973. *Cranial Variation in Man: A Study by Multivariate Analysis of Patterns of Difference Among Recent Human Populations.* Papers of the Peabody Museum of Archaeology and Ethnology, Vol. 67 (Cambridge: Harvard University).

Jolly, C. J., and F. Plog, 1976. *Physical Anthropology and Archaeology* (New York: Alfred A. Knopf).

Kellock, W. L., and P. A. Parsons, 1970. Variation of Minor Non-metrical Skeletal Variants in Australian Aborigines. *American Journal of Physical Anthropology* 32:409–422.

Kowalski, C. J., 1972. A Commentary on the Use of Multivariate Statistical Methods in Anthropometric Research. *American Journal of Physical Anthropology* 36:119–131.

Laughlin, W. S., 1968. The Demography of Hunters: An Eskimo Example. In *Man the Hunter*, R. Lee and I. DeVore, eds. (Chicago: Aldine), pp. 241–249.

Peebles, C. S., 1974. *Moundville: The Organization of a Prehistoric Community and Culture* (Ph.D. diss., University of California, Santa Barbara).

Perzigian, A. J., 1975. Natural Selection on the Dentition of an Arikara Population. *American Journal of Physical Anthropology* 42:63–70.

Robbins, L. M., 1975. The Investigation of Infanticide in an Ohio Fort Ancient Site. (Paper presented at the 40th annual meeting of the Society for American Archaeology, Dallas.)

Stewart, T. D., 1973. *The People of America* (New York: Charles Scribner's Sons).

Washburn, S. L., 1952. The Strategy of Physical Anthropology. In *Anthropology Today: An Encyclopedic Inventory*, A. L. Kroeber, ed. (New York: Wenner-Gren Foundation), pp. 1–14.

The Story of Life Revealed by the Dead

LOUISE M. ROBBINS

ORGANISMS adapt to an environment through the evolution of biological traits or organs that contribute to their survival. With an extrasomatic mechanism like culture, they can manipulate the environment to a degree, to ease their adaptation. Human populations have used culture for thousands of years to combat the selective pressures of their environment; yet for many years, these fundamental premises received little attention from researchers in archeology and cultural history who studied prehistoric populations in the Western hemisphere. For many years—far too many years in the opinion of the critics—physical, or biological, anthropologists concentrated on the description of particular physical traits of prehistoric skeletal series. More specifically, they studied prehistoric crania.

An attempt was made to establish typological categories for human groups that were analogous to the lithic and ceramic categories of the archeologist, and for much the same purpose. It was assumed that the physical "types" that were produced by categorization would provide researchers with definitive knowledge of prehistoric populations and of their geographic distributions, movements, migrations, and admixtures with adjacent groups. Our restricted view of what could be learned from prehistoric skeletons prevented us from recognizing the vast amount of information that the dead offered to us, with regard not only to their physical characteristics, but also to their way of life, their activity and behavioral patterns, and their adaptations to their environments.

Biological anthropologists have come a long way in their studies of prehistoric peoples in America since Hrdlička (1916) studied the Lenape and later compiled his data on the crania of southeastern Indians (Hrdlička 1940), and since Neumann (1952 : 13–34) constructed his typological classification of North American Indians. Within the last fifteen years, a gradual shift away from descriptive studies of skeletal series and their biological affiliations with adjacent populations has occurred (Funkhouser 1939 : 109–126; Hulse 1941 : 57–68; Snow 1948; Stewart 1966 : 67–87). This is not to say that problem-oriented studies were not conducted in the past. Leigh (1925 : 179–196) investigated the relationship of diet and dental attrition; Wakefield and Dellinger (1940: 453–462) and others focused on paleopathologies; and Johnston (1962: 249–254) investigated the aging of immature individuals. Most of these studies, nevertheless, described the biological characteristics and did not pursue their biocultural ramifications.

With these investigative orientations, it is not surprising that biological anthropologists often were—and still are—stereotyped by their anthropology colleagues as being "bone anthropologists" who are "laboratory-centered." It is true that skeletal series were and are yet today often analyzed separately, in isolation from the associated cultural material that the archeologist recovered, but that situation is changing.

What brought about the shift in research interests of biological anthropologists in the past decade or so? We might attribute the shift to a gradual maturing of the physical anthropological profession, an elusive factor to evaluate. It may be attributable to the analytic advancements in the methods and techniques of skeletal examination and in the archeological recovery of prehistoric cultural materials. The latter factors no doubt have greatly influenced our studies, but a more important contributing force seems to stem from the fact that biological anthropologists have begun to ask more questions about the skeletal populations than could be answered by traditional data-gathering techniques.

Metrical dimensions of the skulls provided quantitative data on average head and facial breadths and lengths. They yielded no information, however, on why some crania exhibited deformation and others did not, or why some burial populations contained more males than females, or vice versa. The aim of this effort was to quantify the morphological, or nonmetrical, traits of the individuals who were selected for analysis. (Seldom did the group include all individuals in the series.) The purpose was to obtain a generalized physical description of the population rather than investigate the adaptive significance of the phenotypic variation among the members. Researchers carefully measured various long bones of individuals in a series to estimate the stature of the adults, but they overlooked the effects of diet, nutrition, or disease on statural growth and maintenance. Ironically, each skeleton, whether complete or fragmentary, cleaned or uncleaned, contained a wealth of information, which was ignored, about the life of that individual.

Descriptive studies of skeletal series, or populations, have not been discontinued even today, nor should they be, because properly designed studies can elicit data on microevolutionary biological changes in particular traits within populations and trace the spatial-temporal distribution of the traits. With increasing frequency, though, descriptive studies are now incorporated into larger, more inclusive biocultural research designs that examine the population within its bio-physico-sociocultural context.

As biological anthropologists began the arduous task of unraveling the life stories of their prehistoric human subjects, it soon became evident that they had to communicate their different data needs to archeological colleagues in more explicit terms than had been done in the past. It was also essential to become familiar with various analytic techniques that were being developed and used in nonrelated and even remote disciplines, which occasionally introduced nearly insurmountable communication problems with specialists in those disciplines. Nuclear physicists, biochemists, general dentists, and agronomists, for example, rarely entertain thoughts of prehistoric skeletons, much less of how they can contribute to resolving problems that relate to the skeletons. Some biological anthropologists found that they could not cultivate a full perspective of the many variables that affected either favorably or unfavorably the life and death of prehistoric peoples by sitting in laboratories and studying the skeletons as though they existed in a vacuum, apart from environmental or cultural influences. Hence, they went into the field with the archeologist whenever possible to examine the topographical setting of the cultural site, to study the manner in which the occupants had been buried, and to witness the recovery of cultural and dietary materials.

A basic premise of evolution is that each component of an environment stands in a special relationship with every other component, and a modification in any one part of it will effect some measure of change in every other part. When a prehistoric group, therefore, moved into a geographic area, its presence produced modifications in the natural environment as the people hunted or gathered food. If the people were few in number, their disturbance of the environment might not be notably detrimental. If wattle and daub dwellings were constructed to house even a hundred people, however, and a stockade was built around the houses, significant changes would take place in the environment. These would include loss of trees, loss or reduction of food animals that inhabited the trees or their vicinity, and introduction of grasslands or cultivated fields. All of these changes would then have impact on the human population affecting diet, nutritional shifts, disease potentials, and changing patterns of behavioral activities. It is possible to collect data that demonstrate the adaptive, and maladaptive, responses made by prehistoric peoples to withstand the environmental shifts and daily stresses.

During the past fifteen years, I have examined many prehistoric skeletal populations primarily from the eastern United States. At the outset I, like many before me, used cranial metrical and morphological characteristics to denote degrees of phenotypic similarity and differences be-

tween skeletal series (Robbins 1963). Several aspects of my studies contributed to the broadening of my investigative approach. I questioned
the use of only complete adult male crania for analyses when, by definition, a "population" includes individuals of both sexes and of all ages,
regardless of the condition of their crania. I also questioned the rigorous
cleaning techniques of the skeletal material that produced an aesthet-
ically "clean" bone, but which eliminated future analyses of the soil
adhering to the bones; in many cases, that soil was the last bit of soil
from the site. I recognized phenotypic similarities and differences in
skeletal series from different archeological sites, and I began to look for
the biological *and* cultural causes of the variation (Robbins 1968 : 415–
424).

As I perused archeological reports for information on the pertinent
cultures, I became increasingly aware that archeologists and biological
anthropologists were studying isolated segments of the same phenomenon—human biocultural adaptation in a given ecosystem—but as though
the segments were nonrelated (see Neumann 1937 : 227–264; Collins
1941 : 145–155; Snow 1945 : 87–95; Lewis and Lewis 1961 : 145–173,
among many others pertaining to prehistoric populations in the eastern
United States). I am not suggesting that biological anthropologists and
archeologists stop their research on prehistoric peoples unless the investigators are trained in both fields of study. We must consciously recognize, however, the possible interpretative limitations of our data when
we use them to support or refute generalized statements of prehistoric
human adaptation. Some of my recent work with prehistoric peoples illustrates the points to which I have been alluding.

The people who occupied the Archaic shellmound of Indian Knoll
(Oh 2, Ohio County, Kentucky) are probably as well known as any prehistoric group in the eastern United States. In the fall and winter of 1915
and 1916, C. B. Moore (1916 : 444–448) and his workers excavated
298 burials (183 adults, 23 adolescents, and 92 children and infants)
from the site. Broken skeletons were discarded and pathological specimens were sent to the Army Medical Museum in Washington, D.C. Sixty-
six crania and most of the postcranial bones of some of the individuals
were saved and subsequently sent as a gift to the National Museum at
the Smithsonian Institution (USNM). The disposition of the other burials
that he removed is unknown. Moore also conducted excavations at nine
other sites along the Green River in western Kentucky, and some crania
from those sites were sent with the Indian Knoll series to the National
Museum. One consequence of Moore's practice of combining crania is
that the USNM crania catalogued for the Indian Knoll site actually come
from different stratigraphic depths of different sites along the Green

River (see figure B, plate 3, Stewart and Quade 1969 : 106). I will return to the significance of stratigraphy in those sites later.

The Indian Knoll site was more fully excavated by Webb (1946) in the late 1930's, although flood waters from the Green River prevented complete excavation of the site. Approximately 880 burials were recovered from Indian Knoll during Webb's excavation, and a selected sample of them was subsequently studied by Snow (1948 : 384). He recorded metrical dimensions and indices for the crania and for postcranial bones; pathologies of the teeth and bones were noted; and an Indian Knoll physical "type" was isolated, although a broad range of cranial variation was recognized. Snow postulated that the people had occupied the site for about five hundred years.

In recent years I have had several occasions to reexamine the archeological and skeletal data from Indian Knoll and to reread the literature pertaining to them. Foremost among my findings is that only about 60 percent to 70 percent of the site was excavated. Second, Indian Knoll is a multiple component site which was occupied from the Archaic into the Mississippian cultural period. Third, the phenotypic variation that Snow observed in the crania takes on an added significance when the individuals are placed in their proper cultural context and stratigraphic level. Particular populational patterns emerge when one considers differing skeletal morphologies, distribution of disarticulated burials, cut marks (or butcher marks) on bones, and analysis of individuals who were killed with projectile points. We still must speculate on the number of Indian Knoll females who died during pregnancy or childbirth because bones of many fetuses apparently were not recognized when the burial was excavated. I have found isolated fetal bones that were placed with animal bone fragments and have been able to trace them to particular burials by using the archeological field specimen records.

I recently began an examination of the human skeletal material recovered by Webb and his workers (1950) from another shellmound that is assumed to have been occupied about the same time as the Indian Knoll site, but which is located further along the Green River in Butler County, Kentucky. The people of the Carlson Annis shellmound (Bt 5) had not been examined since they were removed from the site in 1940. Archeological fieldnotes and work progress reports[1] indicate that approximately 30 percent to 35 percent of the site was excavated, from which 389 human burials and 21 dog burials were recovered. Thus, the burials represent only a sample of the population that occupied the site.

"Burial" count illustrates a basic orientational difference between archeologists and biological anthropologists. The number of "burials" does not necessarily equal the number of "individuals" who were recovered during excavation. One "burial" (Bt 5–2), for example, contained three humans (two adults and one adolescent) and one dog. Another example of orientational difference is revealed in the fact that burial numbers may be assigned to individuals whose remains are not saved for analysis, a common occurrence with poorly preserved or fragmentary bones and the bones of young infants. Unless those bones are saved too, it is impossible to investigate the causes of differential bone preservation.

Questions of bone preservation include the following: Was soil acidity or alkalinity the main destructive factor? Was bone age (young versus mature) a factor? Was nutrition or disease a factor? Are some bones, or sections of them, more resistant to destruction than others? In addition to providing answers to questions of bone preservation, all bones—whether fragmentary or not—provide valuable information about the general health of the people, their pathogenic or functional pathologies, functional stresses to which they subjected their bodies, and their cultural behaviors toward their dead.

In 1974 I began working with Patty Jo Watson and her colleagues in the analysis of materials from a previously unexcavated section of the Annis shellmound. The research project was aimed at the recovery of data on the settlement pattern and subsistence of the prehistoric occupants (Marquardt and Watson 1974).[2] Special emphasis was placed on the recovery of particular data from each square meter of the two 2 × 2 meter sections, that is, stratigraphic changes, taxonomic identification, and quantitative distribution of fresh water mussels and gastropods, stratigraphic collection of soil for flotation, and other data. Six human burials and one dog burial (unassociated with a human) were removed from the two sections. The cultural orientation toward treatment of the dead was the same for humans and dogs; that is, each individual was placed in a grave in a particular anatomical position and covered with midden from the site.

My participation in the water flotation of the soil samples (Watson 1976) from the site yielded far more biocultural information about the people than I had anticipated. First, it appears that we may have been too hasty in our assumption that the shellmounds represent year-round habitation sites of a particular population. The dietary debris that is being extracted from the soil by means of flotation seems indicative of intense seasonal occupation. Second, we also may have relied too strongly on the presence of the mussel shell in formulating our interpretations of their primacy as a food source and in our search for causative explanations of extreme dental attrition. According to Meighan (1969: 415–422) and Parmalee and Klippel (1974 : 421–434), the contents of the mussels at the Annis shellmounds would have been too small for a consistent primary food source, i.e., an inequity in energy expended relative to energy received. There is, nevertheless, evidence that shell contents were eaten during prehistoric clambakes and perhaps in a soup that was made in a water-filled skin container heated by the "hot rock" cooking method. Plums, berries, and persimmons were also part of the diet (Yarnell, personal communication); their presence and quantity infer seasonal occupation of the site. The most persistent food debris in the soil is the mixture of charred hickory nut shells and small fish bones, which is followed closely by bones of turtles and small rodents.

To the biological anthropologist, the content and distribution of the dietary remains of the shellmound people provide important clues to their food-gathering activities, division of labor, functional stress markings on the skeletons, and their general state of health. Except for the deer and turkey bones in the midden deposits, the other food items could have been either collected or caught by women and even children. Sexual dimorphism is not distinct in the skeletal remains of males and females; instead, the muscle stress marks and skeletal robusticity of females suggest strenuous physical activities, especially activities that place stress on the head, shoulders, arms, back, and knees. An investigation is now underway to identify bodily movement and activity patterns that could produce comparable skeletal stresses.

At first glance the correlation between dental attrition and the ingestion of food containing abrasive materials seems obvious without extensive study. A closer examination of the alveolar region of crania in the Annis shellmound, however, reveals pathological conditions that would initiate behavioral adjustments in response to masticatory stresses, all of which would affect the form and degree of tooth wear. From the size and shape of the temporo-mandibular fossae and the corresponding mandibular condyles, one can infer masticatory stresses of compression and lateral movements of the mandible. Angulation of the gonial region and the coronoid process also reveals evidence for masticatory stress. The severity of periodontal abscesses, bone destruction, and tooth loss are reflected in the angular changes of wear patterns on the teeth and of stress on the bones. In retrospect, the individual is demonstrating compensatory behavioral adjustments to acute, chronic, or periodic dental pathology.

An inspection of the teeth discloses a rapid rate of tooth attrition which prompted morphological changes in the tooth itself, especially in the root area, with pronounced deposition of secondary cementum on the root surfaces and withdrawal of the neural and nutritional supply to the tooth. The result of the modification amounts to a prehistoric root canal treatment. Dental pathology of maxillary teeth shows a positive correlation with infections in the maxillary sinuses. Hence the extent of dental attrition may be an indicator of whether an individual's state of health permits him or her to function effectively in the population or whether it exposes the person to other debilitating or lethal factors in the environment. A word of caution is offered with respect to attributing all tooth wear to an abrasive diet. I recently discovered that contemporary individuals who chew tobacco also exhibit excessive tooth wear, the pattern of tooth wear reminiscent of prehistoric populations.

Turning to a population from a different geographical environment and a different cultural period, I want to discuss another kind of skeletal pathology and the ramifications of research on this pathology. Several years ago, I examined the overt manifestations of skeletal pathology in a Fort Ancient population (Bb 12, Buckner Site, Bourbon County) from the Inner Blue Grass region of Kentucky (Robbins 1971). Forty-two burials contained the remains of 78 individuals, ranging from fetuses to adults. The archeological data indicated that the people were maize agriculturalists who also hunted some deer and turkey. According to traditional beliefs, an agricultural subsistence is a progressive adaptation over a hunting and gathering economy in terms of human survival and population growth. Prehistoric agriculture enabled people to settle permanently in one area, it provided a reliable source of food, it permitted food surpluses, and it could support more people.

As I examined the people of the Buckner site, I speculated on the possibility that our concept of contemporary agriculture and its benefits might have dulled our awareness of possible maladaptive effects of prehistoric agriculture. Every individual, including the fetal individuals, in the Buckner skeletal series exhibited evidence for some degree of bone or tooth pathology. Nearly all of the bones and teeth of some individuals exhibited the pathological changes, while only particular bones in other individuals were affected. Two approaches could be taken in studying the skeletons. One merely could describe individual pathologies, or one could attempt to place the pathologies in a biocultural, populational perspective. When the latter approach is used, a pattern emerges both in the bodily areas that are afflicted and in the progressive physical deterioration of those areas. In short, a debilitating disease process was active within the population, and the seemingly diverse pathologies in different individuals merely represented different stages of the process. A search through archeological reports that contained skeletal data produced two references to similar disease processes in other populations. Each was a considerable geographic distance from the Buckner people (Brues 1958:27–32; 1959:64–70; Hoyme and Bass 1962:329–400). The probability seemed remote that the pathologies in each of the populations would have the same pathogenic origin, especially in light of their geographic diversity. The populations did have one trait in common, however. They were maize agriculturalists.

I discussed the theory of potential interrelatedness of diet, disease, and environment in the Inner Blue Grass area with an archeologist colleague. He, too, had contemplated the question of environmental interference on the unusually sporadic prehistoric human occupational pattern in the area. Some sites from the Archaic cultural period are found in the Inner Blue Grass region, but Woodland (or Adena) sites are scarce although they are numerous in adjacent geographic areas. Not until the Late Mississippian, or Fort Ancient, cultural period did people inhabit the region on a seemingly permanent basis, and those people were maize agriculturalists like the Buckner group. My colleague and I combined our research efforts in an attempt to unravel the mystery of how the environment could adversely affect human adaptation to the extent that populations shunned it until a suitable food base rendered it livable.

When we initiated the investigation of diet, disease, and environment relationships, we were naively unaware of the complexities we would encounter as we sifted out the variables in the chain-of-life that were applicable to our problem. As our investigation progressed, we became cognizant of the need for the expertise of diverse academic specialists when we pursued various lines of inquiry (Duffield and Robbins 1971). Geologists and geomorphologists provided data for the reconstruction of rock formations, water sources, and topographic features in the area through prehistoric times. Agronomists, soil chemists, and biochemists contributed data on soil composition, soil chemistry, and nutritive values of soils. Botanists supplied information on diversification and on extraction, utilization, and retention of soil nutrients by plants. From the work of vertebrate anatomists and mammalogists, we evaluated the absence, presence, and distribution of fish, birds, and mammals with respect to their potentiality as food sources.

Since the Kentucky Inner Blue Grass lies within the midwestern "goiter belt" (a geographic region that has a deficient level of iodine in soil and water), trace mineral levels in soils, plants, and animals were investigated. Ultimately, the trace minerals were found to be a key link in the whole chain-of-life process, both in terms of initiating and of maintaining processes. Nutritional reports contained ample data on caloric values of food items, some of which were adaptable to prehistoric dietary remains. There was little data, however, on trace mineral ranges: that is, how many of the twenty-two trace minerals are present and in what quantity in food items that were applicable to prehistoric diets. As Duffield and I became better informed on the subtle, yet crucial, effects of trace mineral excesses and deficiencies on the food chain in an environment, we sought nondestructive techniques for trace mineral analyses of prehistoric human bone.[3] Atomic absorption and neutron activational analyses are two techniques used in trace mineral studies by chemists who have access to radioactive sources (atomic reactors). The former technique requires that some bone be sacrificed for the analysis; the latter technique operates along the principle of the laser beam and hence is often regarded as a "nondestructive" process. However, trace mineral levels and distribution in bone, or in different parts of a single bone, can be obtained by either of the analytic techniques.[4]

Duffield and I have not terminated our investigations, but preliminary findings have important bearing on prehistoric adaptation in certain geographic regions (Duffield and Robbins 1973). While the blue grass of Kentucky may be a superior food source for race horses today, during prehistoric times the soils apparently lacked some necessary nutrients, or quantities of those nutrients, to support a broad diversity of plants. Animals avoided the area because of the scarce food source, and early prehistoric peoples followed their own food base, the animals. Not until an extra food-producing mechanism, agriculture, was introduced into the area, could a population like the one at the Buckner site settle there for any length of time. Some members could make hunting expeditions outside the Blue Grass area, while others remained behind to tend crops and collect the little food the environment had to offer. The deficiency of particular minerals in the soils, especially zinc and manganese, and the emphasis on maize as an important if not primary source of food combined to effect subtle but significant changes in the health of the people. There is a sharp increase in dental pathology in the form of periodontal and alveolar bone destruction, numerous caries with subsequent abscesses and tooth loss, and carious destruction of deciduous teeth before permanent teeth appear. Individuals responded to the stress of their chronic dental pathologies by continually readjusting their masticatory pattern, which is reflected in the various angular planes of cusp wear and in bone erosion of the temporo-mandibular joint.

Skeletal pathologies of the Buckner site followed a particular pattern of destructive action and a similar pattern in its spread from one part of the body to another. In the initial stages, periosteal rarification and secondary bone deposition occur on the tibial shafts. Gradually the ribs, clavicles, and vertebrae exhibit the surface rarification, but with lessened secondary deposition of bone. As the cranium, bones of the arms, and femora manifest periosteal destruction, the other bones are undergoing erosion of both the periosteal and endosteal cortical layers concomitant with trabecular deposition in the medullary cavity. The spongy trabecular bone gradually fills the cavity. The compact cortical bone loses some of its tensile strength as it undergoes the thinning process and becomes susceptible to damage in the more active individuals. Bones like ribs and clavicles, for example, exhibit sequential fractures or breaks and healings with a gradual distortion of bone morphology accompanying the stress condition. Comparable traumas occur in other parts of the body. Collapse of the thoracic and lumbar vertebral bodies and their separation from the neural arch and spine are widespread in the population.

The disease process is more severely expressed in some individuals than in others at the Buckner site, but it is visibly present to some degree in all individuals. I have subsequently found evidence for the same disease process in prehistoric groups who lived outside the Blue Grass area; in the preliminary data now available, a positive correlation (on the order of 0.87) exists between the disease manifestation and maize agriculture. Other potentially intervening variables are still being investigated, however. The adaptational benefits that we associated with prehistoric agriculture, nonetheless, seem dubious. Members of agricultural groups become targets for pathogens of epidemic proportions, food shortages, nutritional deficiencies, stresses of crowding and the intensification of social interactions. Any or all of these factors might not be fatal to the individual but could seriously impair his or her functional productivity.

The biological anthropologist rarely has an opportunity to participate in the archeological recovery of the sociocultural data associated with skeletal data that he or she assesses from a site. The sociocultural information, however, may reveal cultural behaviors that directly influence the biological configuration of the population. I am working now with archeologists in Ohio in an attempt to reconstruct the biocultural environment of the Late Woodland (or Fort Ancient) people who inhabited a village between A.D. 1100 and 1250 (Heilman and Robbins 1974). This site is known as the Incinerator site. An examination of the skeletal remains reveals who died—adult, adolescent, child, or infant—and whether they are male or female, when sex can be determined.

The soil surrounding a burial (the burial "fill") also produces evidence for approximating the particular time of year in which the individual was buried, and possibly died. If macroscopic evidence is not recovered from the burial fill, a sample of the fill is collected for future flotational and palynological analyses concerning seasonality. A soil sample from within the chest cavity is collected for a similar analysis. Soil is also being collected from within the pelvic cavity in an attempt to recover the remains of intestinal food wastes still preserved in the soil. The cultural items buried with an individual are carefully noted and described and their precise context is noted relative to the skeleton. Their presence, absence, diversity, composition, and number convey subtle sociocultural information about behavioral activities. Examples of these sociocultural data include indicators of possible family and village statuses and ranks. An exacting record is kept of the shape, size, associated materials (limestone slabs, for instance), and orientation of the grave or pit, of the way in which the individual was placed in the grave, and of where the grave is positioned relative to other graves, dwellings, storage pits, and so on.

When sociocultural and biological data on burials are combined and then examined in conjunction with the archeological data on the remainder of the site, the investigators can recognize more fully the interrelationship of the aspects and the influence of each on that prehistoric society. The data collection and analysis is far from complete for the Incinerator site people, but some definite biocultural relationships are emerging, and other behaviors may be inferred from them.

Settlement pattern is one of the areas of investigation and hypothetical reconstruction. Wattle and daub dwellings apparently surrounded a central plaza. It appears that each dwelling faced the plaza because each one has an unobstructed path through the storage pit and burial areas to the plaza. Each house apparently had its own nuclear or extended family burial plot situated between the house and the plaza and separated from adjacent family plots by undisturbed soil. According to the burial data, some households, or families, contained more members than others, and according to the records on burial goods, there were differential status positions among members within a household as well as status differences between households. While there is a consistent pattern in the burial ritual of grave preparation and interment within family plots, subtle differences occur between plots. For example, some family groups were less meticulous than others in digging the grave of adequate size and width for the body and in positioning the body within the grave.

The data for some graves suggest that the grave had been dug for a person other than the one interred in it. Some graves are much too large and others too small for the individual in them. One might speculate that the person for whom the grave was intended recovered from a serious illness (and there is sufficient pathology to infer periodic critical illnesses). The grave was used for a subsequent death in, we assume on the basis of present data, that family group.

Perhaps the most significant bit of information that is being recovered from the burial data of the Incinerator people pertains to the practices of infanticide and possible intentional abortion, cultural practices of which heretofore we have had no reliable evidence for prehistoric groups (Robbins 1975). Factors contributing to the deduction of infanticide and intentional abortion include irregularities in burial ritual, spatial placement of burials, and attendant behaviors toward deceased individuals. Fetal bones appear at various depths in midden pits; some bones are so small (early fetal age) that, without careful attention to their diagnostic human form, they might be classed as animal bones. Several young adult females died during an early stage of pregnancy, but we can not determine with certainty with present methods of assessment whether death resulted from an attempted unsuccessful abortion, which failed to eject the fetus, or from other possibly related causes. The analysis of those individuals has not been completed.

The evidence for infanticide is derived from several behavioral characteristics of the Incinerator people. It was noted earlier that each household had a burial plot, and the plot contained the remains of infants and children as well as adolescents and adults. Infant twins were even recovered from one plot. In these plots, the youngsters were accorded the same burial ritual as the adults. Graves were prepared for them, special attention was given to the placement of the body in the grave (positioning of head, arms, and legs), and grave goods often accompanied the child. However, not all infants were placed in the household plot; instead, some infants were "buried" behind the houses near the stockade that surrounded the village. Thus far we have found only one infant who was buried in a shallow grave in the corner of a house.

At first glance, these isolated burials might not seem unusual and would not be interpreted as unusual if they were examined in a laboratory away from the cultural data. The isolated burials, however, share several features that stand out in contrast to the infant burials in household plots. Little care was given to the preparation of the isolated grave; it tended to be shallow and ill-defined. The individual often was made to fit the grave, which resulted in a strange body alignment or nonalignment. Little attempt seems to have been made to position the body. On the contrary, according to the distribution of individual bones it appears that the body was tossed into the grave and covered with nearby soils. Close examination of the individuals reveals one other common feature. The isolated individuals that have been examined so far exhibit "green bone" (that is, fresh bone) cranial depression fractures, usually in the parietal area, that could not have resulted from the gradual pressures exerted on the crania from the weight of burial fill.

While there is substantial evidence for infanticide, part of the evidence suggests ceremonial sacrifice as a causative factor for the death of certain infants. Those individuals are recovered from the bottom of food storage pits adjacent to a large dwelling structure at one end of the plaza that is set slightly apart from the household dwellings. That this dwelling belonged to the village leader, or chief, is still being investigated, but the evidence seems to support this hypothesis. The "sacrificed" infants also share a common trait. They were dropped or thrown into the storage pits head first, a deduction based on the settling of the postcranial bones around the skull as the flesh decayed from the bones.

A question arises relative to infanticide, which concerns the sex of the victim, because preference of one sex over the other could affect the sex ratio of the population. An unbalanced ratio of males to females could, for instance, intensify the stresses of sociocultural adaptation within the population. An example of this would be the availability of mates; another, the establishment of family units and households. Ultimately, sexual preference in infanticide can affect the genetic composition of the population, even if only on a microevolutionary level. As research continues on the Incinerator people, special efforts are being made to recover precise data that contribute to the identification of specific biocultural interrelationships.

In the course of this paper I have attempted to identify the broad variety of information that can be obtained from the study of prehistoric populations. I do not pretend that the use of these methodological approaches will enable us to reconstruct fully the biocultural environments of past populations, but they move us far closer to that goal than we have ever been before. Biological anthropologists who focused specifically on the metrical and morphological characteristics of a population collected data on only one isolated aspect of the biocultural individuals in that population. The archeologists collected data on still another isolated segment of the total human being in a cultural environment.

Ironically, we highly specialized scientists have been slow to recognize the vast legacy left to us by the prehistoric peoples. The legacy is biocultural information, not either biological or cultural information alone. From the analysis of skeletal remains, one can deduce many cultural features, including dietary habits, activity patterns, response to injury, disease, and stress, cultural influences on gene frequency, and many others. In the same line of inquiry, many biological characteristics can be inferred from material cultural items—food remains and divisions of labor; food remains and activity patterns for collection and processing food items; pottery-making or lithic manufacture and structural stresses on the body, diet, and affinitive disease, and others. The prehistoric people have demonstrated how they adapted to their environment by leaving the configurations of their sites—placement of hearths, storage pits and dwellings, as well as a variety of food debris, distribution of lithic debitage. They have also demonstrated this adaptive process by indicating their treatment of the dead, and even by revealing their approximate age at the time of death. Our task is to examine, analyze, and interpret the adaptations of these populations using the same frame of reference in which they lived—the biocultural frame.

NOTES

1. The fieldnotes and work progress reports on the Carlson Annis site are on file in the University of Kentucky skeletal storage building in Lexington, Ky.
2. The Watson and Marquardt Shell Mound Archaeological Project (SMAP) was partially funded by a grant to Watson from the National Geographic Society.
3. See the *Proceedings* of the annual conference on trace substances in environmental health published each year since 1967 by the University of Missouri, Columbia, Mo.
4. Editor's note: see Gilbert's discussion of trace element research methods.

REFERENCES

Brues, A. M., 1958. Skeletal Material from the Horton Site. *Bulletin, Oklahoma Anthropological Society* 6 : 27–32.

————, 1959. Skeletal Material from the Morris Site (CK–39). *Bulletin, Oklahoma Anthropological Society* 7 : 63–70.

Collins, H. B., Jr., 1941. Relationships of an Early Indian Cranial Series from Louisiana. *Journal of Washington Academy of Sciences* 31 : 145–155.

Duffield, L. F., and L. M. Robbins, 1971. Environmental Influences on Bone Pathology: A Study of the Fort Ancient in the Kentucky Inner Blue Grass Region. (Manuscript on file, Department of Anthropology, University of Kentucky.)

————, 1973. Mn Deficiency: A Prehistoric Disease? (Paper presented at the 38th annual meeting of the Society for American Archaeology, San Francisco.)

Funkhouser, W. D., 1939. A Study of the Physical Anthropology and Pathology of the Osteological Material from the Wheeler Basin. *Bureau of American Ethnology, Bulletin* 122 : 109–126.

Heilman, J. M., and L. M. Robbins, 1974. Incinerator Site (33My57), A Possible Fort Ancient Frontier Site. (Paper presented at the 39th annual meeting of the Society for American Archaeology, Washington, D.C.)

Hoyme, L. C., and W. M. Bass, 1962. Human Skeletal Remains from the Tollifer (Ha6) and Clarksville (Mc14) Sites, John H. Kerr Reservoir Basin, Virginia. *Bureau of American Ethnology, Bulletin* 182 : 329–340.

Hrdlička, A., 1916. Physical Anthropology of the Lenape or Delawares and of the Eastern Indians in General. *Bureau of American Ethnology, Bulletin* 62 : entire bulletin.

——, 1940. Catalogue of Human Crania in the United States National Museum Collections: Indians of the Gulf States. *Proceedings of the National Museum, Smithsonian Institution* 87 : 315–464.

Hulse, F. S., 1941. The People Who Lived at Irene. In *Irene Mound Site, Chatham County, Georgia,* by J. Caldwell and C. McCann (Athens: University of Georgia Press), pp. 57–68.

Johnston, F. E., 1962. Growth of the Long Bones of Infants and Young Children at Indian Knoll. *American Journal of Physical Anthropology* 20 : 249–254.

Leigh, R. W., 1925. Dental Pathology of Indian Tribes of Varied Environments and Food Conditions. *American Journal of Physical Anthropology* 8 : 179–196.

Lewis, T. M. N., and M. K. Lewis, 1961. *Eva, an Archaic Site.* (Knoxville: University of Tennessee Press).

Marquardt, W. H., and P. J. Watson, 1974. The Green River, Kentucky, Shellmound Archaeological Project. (Paper presented at the 73rd annual meeting of the American Anthropological Association, Mexico City).

Meighan, C. E., 1969. Molluscs as Food Remains in Archaeological Sites. In *Science in Archaeology*, D. Brothwell and E. Higgs, eds. (New York: Praeger), pp. 415–422.

Moore, C. B., 1916. Some Aboriginal Sites on Green River, Kentucky. *Journal of the Academy of Natural Sciences of Philadelphia*, 2nd ser., 16 : 432–511.

Neumann, G. K., 1937. Preliminary Notes on the Crania from Fulton County, Illinois. In *Rediscovering Illinois*, Fay-Cooper Cole and T. Deuel, eds. (Chicago: University of Chicago Press), pp. 227–264.

——, 1952. Archeology and Race in the American Indian. In *Archeology of Eastern United States.* J. B. Griffin, ed. (Chicago: University of Chicago Press), pp. 13–34.

Parmalee, P. W., and W. E. Klippel, 1974. Freshwater Mussels as a Prehistoric Food Source. *American Antiquity* 39 : 421–434.

Robbins, L. M., 1963. Physical and Cultural Relationships of the Late Archaic Red Ocher People of the Illinois Valley (M.A. thesis, Indiana University).

——, 1968. The Identification of the Prehistoric Shawnee Indians (Ph.D. diss., Indiana University).

——, 1971. The High Incidence of Bone Pathologies in Fort Ancient Peoples in Kentucky. (Paper presented at the 40th annual meeting of the American Association of Physical Anthropologists, Boston.)

——, 1975. The Investigation of Infanticide in an Ohio Fort Ancient Site. (Paper presented at the 40th annual meeting of the Society for American Archaeology, Dallas.)

Snow, C. E., 1945. Tchefuncte Skeletal Remains. In *The Tchefuncte Culture, an Early Occupation of the Lower Mississippi Valley*, by J. A. Ford and G. I. Quimby, Jr., *Memoirs of the Society for American Archaeology*, No. 2, pp. 87–95.

————, 1948. Indian Knoll Skeletons. *Reports in Anthropology* (Lexington: University of Kentucky Press) IV, No. 3, Pt. II.

Stewart, T. D., 1966. Notes on the Human Bones Recovered from Burials in the McLean Mound, North Carolina. *Southern Indian Studies* 18 : 67–87.

Stewart, T. D., and L. G. Quade, 1969. Lesions of the Frontal Bone in American Indians. *American Journal of Physical Anthropology* 30 : 89–110.

Wakefield, E. G., and S. C. Dellinger, 1940. Diseases of Prehistoric Americans of South Central United States. *Ciba Symposia* 2 : 453–462.

Watson, P. J., 1976. In Pursuit of Prehistoric Subsistence: Theoretical and Methodological Implications of Flotation Techniques. *Mid Continental Journal of Archaeology* 1 : in press.

Webb, W. S., 1946. Indian Knoll Site, Oh 2, Ohio County, Kentucky. *Reports in Anthropology and Archaeology* (Lexington: University of Kentucky Press), IV, No. 3. Pt. I.

————, 1950. The Carlson Annis Mound. *Reports in Anthropology* (Lexington: University of Kentucky Press), VII, No. 4.

Middle Mississippian:
A Prehistoric Cultural System Viewed from
a Biological Perspective

DAVID J. WOLF

ARCHEOLOGISTS have for almost a century been excavating and studying prehistoric cultural remains which are known today as "Mississippian." The term *Mississippian* has been used to denote a geographical region, a stage, a phase, an horizon, a period, a pattern, a single culture, as well as a series of cultures in time and space. Through interpretations of excavated data, archeologists have attempted to explain not only the origins and development of material cultural artifacts identified as Mississippian, but also the overall cultural and biological histories of the people who were responsible for those cultural remains. Numerous sites have been excavated in hopes of recovering information that would permit a reconstruction of those histories. The end product of a century of archeological research is a number of complex regional sequences containing detailed descriptions of the material cultural remains. Attempts to ascertain who were the practitioners of Mississippian culture have generally not been successful—with the possible exceptions of linking the historic Natchez with certain prehistoric Mississippian remains (Quimby 1942; Neitzel 1965) and tracing the historic Shawnee to the Fort Ancient Aspect (Griffin 1952 and 1967).

Among the current interpretations of the Mississippian phenomenon, three are being seriously considered in the literature. These three interpretations are:

(1) A single Mississippian culture was developed in the Central Mississippi River Valley by a single biological group. Over time, this population increased in size and migrated to other areas in the Southeast. Eventually, this group supplanted other cultures and populations throughout the area.

(2) Mississippian culture was developed in the Central Mississippi River Valley by a single group. Over time, this culture spread to other groups. Implicit in this interpretation is the assumption that the culture

was borrowed or imposed by conquest upon a series of indigenous populations.

(3) Mississippian culture can also be explained as a series of cultures that were developed by different groups more or less independently and simultaneously.

One other interpretation is possible, although I have not seen it discussed in the literature. The development of Mississippian culture could have been the result of a combination of any or all of these processes.

Support for each of these interpretations can be found in the discussions of the material cultural remains and behavior patterns reflected in the archeological record. In the interpretation of the Mississippian cemetery at the Schild site (Illinois), which contained nearly three hundred Mississippian skeletons, Perino (1971 : 140) considers these Mississippians to have been Late Woodland people who were acculturated into the "Mississippian way of life" being practiced by their neighboring Cahokians.

To the north and east of Cahokia, the Dickson Mounds site has received considerable archeological attention. From the twelve superimposed mounds, a total of 1,039 skeletons has been exposed (Harn 1971). Culturally, the Dickson Mounds were utilized as a cemetery by two distinct groups, as evidenced by the Sepo Late Woodland component and the "classic" Middle Mississippian component. Based upon intrasite multivariate and univariate comparisons of the adult male crania, Blakely (1976 : 32) concludes that ". . . the Late Woodland and Middle Mississippian populations were relatively distinct and since the Sepo sample represents the earlier inhabitants, it seems probable that the Mississippians were immigrants into the Fulton County area . . . they most likely migrated from the Cahokia area."

The second largest Mississippian ceremonial center is located at Moundville, Alabama. Moundville, situated upon the banks of the Black Warrior River, also has been the object of considerable archeological interest (DeJarnette 1952; Peebles 1971). Although little has been published on the work conducted at Moundville—including data for more than three thousand unearthed skeletons—it is apparent that the proper Mississippian traits occur here. It has been suggested by Coe (personal communication) that Moundville may represent yet another site at which there was a direct migration of peoples into the Southeast from the Central Mississippi River Valley.

With regard to Georgia, one again reads about Mississippian migrations and/or invasions (Fairbanks 1952 : 294; Griffin 1967 : 189), but this time into the Macon Plateau region. Within the Macon Plateau area, such sites as Etowah and Ocmulgee Fields are of primary importance.

In the ceramic sequences at these sites and others in the general area there is some support for the migration interpretation. In this region, the historic Creeks are considered to be related to prehistoric Mississippian culture. However, it has not been clearly identified, except on the basis of stamped pottery, whether the Creeks were the "invaders" or the subsequent indigenous "reconquerors." Despite the fact that more than 350 burials were excavated at Etowah and probably a comparable number were excavated at Ocmulgee Fields, there exists little published data concerning the Mississippian skeletal materials recovered from these sites.

In the above discussion, I have attempted to summarize very briefly some of the interpretations of Mississippian culture through a review of various data, inferences, and interpretations obtained from the archeological work. During a review of the archeological literature, a major problem was encountered. Important sites (e.g., Town Creek, North Carolina; Moundville, Alabama; Etowah, Georgia; Kincaid, as well as Cahokia, Illinois) have not been reported upon fully.

The literature contains some information for only a few geographically widely scattered collections recovered from smaller Mississippian sites. The principal collections for which published information is available are summarized in table 1.

Table 1.
Literature Containing Biological Data
for Skeletal Collections from a Mississippian Context

Mississippian Skeletal Collections	Sample Size	Location	Investigator(s) & Date of Publication or Analysis
Menard Mound	4	Arkansas Co., Arkansas	Hrdlička (1908)
Greer Cemetery	8	Jefferson Co., Arkansas	Hrdlička (1908)
Boytt's Field	36	Union Co., Arkansas	Hrdlička (1909)
Irene Mound	265	Chatham Co., Georgia	Hulse (1941)
Koger's Island (Complex 2)	20	Lauderdale Co., Alabama	Newman and Snow (1942) Lane (1969)
Kane Burial Mounds	87	Madison Co., Illinois	Melbye (1963)
Dickson Mounds	17*	Fulton Co., Illinois	Neumann (1937)
	17*		Harn (1971)
	68*		Blakely (1976)

* Indicates that only adult males were analyzed.

In addition to the scattered reports in the literature, at least ten major skeletal collections are known by this author to have partially survived the onslaught of time. These include the collections from the Schild site, the Kane Burial Mounds, and the Dickson Mounds in Illinois; the collections from the Hazel, Vernon Paul, and Upper Nodena sites in Arkansas; the Chuckalissa collection from Memphis, Tennessee; the Moundville, Alabama, collection; and the Etowah and Irene Mound collections from Georgia. Although other collections probably exist, these skeletal collections, because of their relative sizes and completeness, could provide answers to some of the questions about the biological nature of Mississippian groups.

Ideally, all skeletal data recovered from a Mississippian context should be examined in attempting to ascertain which, if any, of the archeological interpretations is correct. However, for pragmatic reasons this is not feasible. Therefore, I will examine in detail some of the available biological data in a test of the validity of the migration interpretation. Skeletal data from the Kane Burial Mounds, as well as the Hazel, Vernon Paul, and Upper Nodena sites, were available to this author. In addition, published information for the Dickson Mounds materials (Blakely 1976) and the Irene Mound site (Hulse 1941) will be employed to test the migration interpretation. Archeologically, it appears that the skeletal collections from these six sites represent similar "social classes." The social classes represented at each of these sites are neither the truly "elite" nor the "peasants," but probably "middle classes," presumably composed of artisans, craftsmen, merchants, and lesser political figures.

Before discussing the actual test of the migration interpretation, some general comments about the archeological contexts from which these six skeletal samples were obtained are in order. The Kane Burial Mounds are located on the high bluffs bordering the American Bottoms. The Kane site, located directly east of the Mitchell site and just north of "downtown" Cahokia, is, in the opinion of this author, a part of the greater urban complex of Cahokia with its eighty-five mounds, its plazas, and large associated village. In addition to proximity, the grave goods and burial orientations suggest Cahokia affiliation. Melbye (1963:7–9) suggested that the individuals interred at the Kane site represent a social class beneath the "elite" buried within the ceremonial centers of Mitchell and Cahokia and a class above the "peasants" buried beneath the house floors of the neighboring farmsteads and hamlets.

All three northeastern Arkansas sites (Hazel, Vernon Paul, and Upper Nodena) represent moderate-sized ceremonial centers along the western floodplain of the Mississippi River. These ceremonial centers, with temple mounds and plazas, had associated villages and cemeteries. The houses were arranged in "wards" that resemble, in form, a modern city block. Distinct cemetery areas were associated with these organized villages (Morse 1973 : 71). The recovered archeological data indicate that the Hazel, Vernon Paul, and Upper Nodena sites supported fairly large populations for at least one hundred years. Also, it appears that the occupations at these sites were contemporaneous, or at least that they overlapped.

To briefly summarize, the skeletal data to be utilized in this paper are outlined in table 2. These data, recorded for skeletons recovered from various geographical locations throughout the Southeast, will be used to test the validity of one of the several interpretations concerning who were the practitioners of Mississippian culture.

Due to the limited scope of this paper, most of the details concerning the methodologies employed in assigning age and sex estimates to the 980 skeletons composing the total sample, as well as the nature of all of the controls that were imposed upon these data to insure reliability and comparability, must be omitted from this discussion. Generally speaking, the widest range of methods possible was employed during the preliminary analyses of the four unreported collections. Aging criteria included pubic symphysis development (McKern and Stewart 1957; Gilbert and McKern 1973), dental development (Schour and Massler 1941; Diamond 1952), epiphyseal union (McKern and Stewart 1957; Krogman 1962) and others. Sexing criteria included innominate morphology (Krogman 1962; Phenice 1969; Bass 1971), intrasample cranial morphology, as well as other features of the postcranial skeleton. Among the more important controls are age (only adults were examined), sex (the sexes were treated separately), deformity (artificially deformed crania were treated independently), and pathology (pathological specimens were omitted). More detailed discussions of the methodologies employed and the controls imposed have been reported elsewhere (Wolf 1976). These six skeletal collections represent at least a 10 percent sample, and in some cases a 50 to 60 percent sample, of the "burial populations" recovered from these sites. Based upon numerous details of the specific archeological contexts, these samples are probably representative of the populations occupying the respective sites.

If the migration interpretation were the correct one, one would expect to find, on the basis of random and representative samples, minimal biological (genetic) differences among the groups from various geographical regions in the Southeast. Few differences would be observed, that is, if the migrant groups were truly representative of the parent population from which they emigrated and if microevolutionary change (particularly genetic drift, gene flow, and selection) did not occur to any signifi-

Table 2.
The Age and Sex Structure of the Six Skeletal Samples

Site	Sex Estimate	Age Estimate						Total Sample Size
		Adult (25+)	Young Adult (15–25)	Adolescent (10–14)	Child (2–9)	Infant (X–1)	Indeterminate	
Hazel (A.D. 1300–1450)	Male	57	25					154
	Female	26	27	2				
	Indeterminate			1	11	5		
Vernon Paul (A.D. 1400–1550)	Male	26	12	2				86
	Female	19	11	1				
	Indeterminate				9	6		
Upper Nodena (A.D. 1400–1500)	Male	34	13					90
	Female	28	13					
	Indeterminate			1	1			
Kane (A.D. 1100–1200)	Male	36	21	1				147
	Female	30	16					
	Indeterminate	2		5	24	6	6	
Dickson Mounds (A.D. 1000–1300)	Male	59	7	1				240
	Female	47	23	6	1			
	Indeterminate			3	45	46	2	
Irene (A.D. 1300–1550)	Male	49	16	4				263
	Female	41	24	6			1	
	Indeterminate	11	7	2	28	6	68	
Total	Male	261	94	8	0	0	0	980
	Female	191	114	15	1	0	1	
	Indeterminate	13	7	12	118	69	76	

Note: Age scaling in years does not apply to the Irene sample. Hulse (1941) simply classified an individual as either adult, young adult, child, etc. Presumably, Hulse's more general categories approximate those employed by this author.

cant degree after the groups migrated. Two crucial questions emerge: "To what degree are the various groups throughout the Southeast biologically related?" and, "How do we measure those relationships?"

As geneticists have repeatedly documented, there are two major sources of phenotypic variation—the environment and genetic structure, including the single gene and polygenic components. The environment alone is responsible, in some instances, for the observed phenotypic variation (for example, types of artificial cranial deformation). In other instances, the possession of certain alleles at a single locus is responsible for a given phenotypic trait. Many, if not most, discrete dental and skeletal traits are considered to be inherited in a Mendelian or epigenetic fashion (Corruccini 1974 and 1976). However, with only a few exceptions, accurate genetic information is not available for the majority of discrete phenotypic traits in the human skeleton. It has also been demonstrated that both the environment and the polygenic component of genetic structure interact to produce observable phenotypic variation in the human skeleton. But in this case, even less information is available about the loci and alleles controlling these continuous traits. Metric dimensions are generally considered to be the result of this kind of interaction (Corruccini 1974 and 1976).

Because each genetic component is known to influence or directly control the expression of a large number of phenotypic characteristics in the human skeleton, it would seem logical that, working from the phenotypic data under controlled circumstances, we should be able to infer the underlying genetic structures of the various groups. And by comparing these structures among the groups, we should be able to provide at least a crude measure of biological relationship among the groups. At least this is the justification for conducting all microevolutionary studies—including those for extant groups.

Discrete traits as an indirect means of phenotypically measuring the single gene component of genetic structure offer at least three advantages. First, phenotypic traits that are inherited as single gene traits are easily observed and measured. They are either present or absent, if penetrance is complete. Another advantage of single gene traits is that they are not, generally, environmentally influenced. And finally, if the phenotypic expression is truly the result of Mendelian inheritance, and pleiotropism is not operating, these traits will be independent of each other. Berry and Berry (1967), Kellock and Parsons (1970), Benfer (1970), Bang and Hasund (1972), and others have generally concluded that the majority of discrete osteological traits are independent. Corruccini (1974) concluded that significant correlations do exist among some hypostotic and hyperstotic traits.[1] His results appear to confirm those of

Ossenberg (1969 and 1970). It does appear that clusters of discrete traits are independent of each other.

Among the disadvantages of employing single gene traits to measure genetic structure are the problems of ascertainment and low frequencies. Without genealogical information, it is difficult to be certain whether the observed phenotypic attribute is the result of the inheritance of alleles at a given locus or the result of a phenocopy.[2] Also, the alleles responsible for the expression of a discrete trait are often present in extremely low frequencies so that, by chance alone, the presence of the trait may not be observed in a given sample.

The advantages offered by continuous variables as the phenotypic means for measuring the polygenic component of genetic structure are two-fold. These features, singly or in various combinations, are what I would term "universal and vital characteristics"—everyone had a head, arms, or legs, but not everyone had or needed an os Inca.[3] The other advantage is that these variables are recorded as interval or ratio scaled variables. Traits scaled in this fashion permit a greater variety of statistical analyses to be performed upon them. However, there are two significant disadvantages in employing such complex phenotypic traits to measure genetic structure. It is difficult to identify and quantify the environmental contribution to the final phenotypic expression of such traits. Also, we cannot, as yet, identify the genes and alleles comprising the polygenic component and can only infer their existence. In other words, we are not exactly sure what it is that we are measuring in such a precise fashion.

Although there has been considerable debate over which type of phenotypic traits and, therefore, which underlying genetic component is the better measure of genetic structure (Ossenberg 1969; Rightmire 1972; Jantz 1973; Berry 1974; Corruccini 1974; and others), I chose to investigate both components, insofar as the available data permit. Each component measures a different aspect of genetic structure and would, therefore, serve as a more or less independent check on the other. Also, because of the highly fragmentary nature of prehistoric skeletal remains it is improbable that we will ever obtain complete characterizations of either component. In combination, we are more likely to achieve a representative sampling of the total genetic structure of a given group than is possible by sampling either component alone.

For these reasons, data were collected for 58 metric traits and 74 discrete traits for the skeletons from the four unreported samples (Hazel, Vernon Paul, Upper Nodena, and Kane sites). At the time of the analyses, comparable data for the Dickson Mounds and Irene Mound site samples were available in the reports for only twenty-two metric variables. These data were present in the form of sample sizes, means, and standard deviations for each variable. The data utilized in various analyses are summarized in table 3. These data represent the minimal numbers of variables employed in the various analyses.

As indicated previously, the primary objective of this paper is to test the validity, with biological data, of the conclusion that the distribution of Mississippian cultural remains is the result of the movements of groups belonging to a single biological population. The analytical procedures and techniques employed to ascertain the degree of biological relationships among the various Mississippian groups (represented by the six skeletal samples) include aspects of both the univariate and multivariate approaches. A series of five separate, but interrelated, hypotheses were

Table 3.
Minimal Number of Data Categories Available for Analysis

Discrete Variables	
Auditory Tori	Posterior Malar Foramina
Mandibular Tori	Accessory Lesser Palatine Foramina
Coronal Ossicles	Hypoglossal Canal Double Foramina
Lambdoidal Ossicles	Double Mental Foramina
Epiteric Ossicles	Supraorbital Notch
Asterionic Ossicles	Parietal Notch Bone
Accessory Infraorbital Foramina	Squamo-Parietal Suture Closed
Zygo-Facial Foramina	Petro-Squamosal Suture Open
Supraorbital Foramina	Mylo-Hyoid Bridging
Frontal Foramina	External Frontal Sulcus
Parietal Foramina	Os Inca
Mastoid Foramina	Os Apicus
Posterior Condylar Canal Foramina	Torus Palatinus
Huschke Foramina	Metopic Suture Open

Metric Variables	
Cranial Length	Palatal Length
Cranial Breadth	Palatal Breadth
Cranial Height	Bicondylar Breadth
Minimum Frontal Breadth	Cranial Index
Bizygomatic Breadth	Cranial Length-Height Index
Total Facial Height	Cranial Breadth-Height Index
Upper Facial Height	Total Facial Index
Nasal Height	Upper Facial Index
Nasal Breadth	Nasal Index
Left Orbital Breadth	Left Orbital Index
Left Orbital Height	Palatal Index

tested to determine whether or not the six skeletal samples were obtained from one population. These five test situations included:

Test Situation No. 1: The univariate approach employing 58 metric variables was used to test the validity of pooling the three Arkansas samples (Hazel, Vernon Paul, and Upper Nodena) into one regional sample.

Based upon the results of *t* tests and *F* tests for significant differences in sample means (at the 5 percent level) for each of the metric variables among the adult males and adult females from the three Arkansas sites, the null hypothesis that no significant differences existed was provisionally accepted. Only three significant differences were recorded for males and only two significant differences were recorded for females. By chance alone, we would expect at least two significant differences to be observed for each sex.

Test Situation No. 2: The univariate approach employing 29 metric variables was used to test the validity of pooling the Kane Mounds and Dickson Mounds samples into one regional Illinois sample.

Again, *t* tests for significant differences in sample means measured at the 5 percent level were computed for the adult males from the Kane and Dickson samples. Of the 29 variables tested, a total of nine significant differences were recorded. On the basis of these differences, the null hypothesis that these male samples were obtained from a single population was rejected. In this instance, it would not be legitimate to pool the Kane and Dickson Mounds samples into a regional Illinois sample.

Test Situation No. 3: The univariate approach employing 22 metric variables was used to test the validity of pooling the combined Arkansas sample, the Kane sample, the Dickson Mounds sample, and the Irene sample into a single Mississippian sample.

The adult females and/or males from each of the four regional samples were compared in terms of significant differences in sample means (with *t* values considered significant at the 5 percent level). Significant differences were recorded for all combinations of sites and sexes. These differences ranged from a low of 5 between the Arkansas females and the Irene females to a high of 16 significant differences between the Arkansas and Dickson males. Based on the weight of the evidence, the null hypothesis that the four regional samples were obtained from a single population was rejected. The consistent pattern of differences, as measured by the univariate approach, fails to support the interpretation that a single biological population was responsible for the existence of Mississippian culture throughout the Southeast.

Test Situation No. 4: The multivariate approach employing 58 metric variables was used to measure biological distance between the three Arkansas and the Kane Mounds samples.

A series of six stepwise discriminant function analyses was performed upon these data with the controlling variables of site, sex, and absence of cranial deformation imposed. The primary statistical objective of the S P S S discriminant function analysis is to maximize the distance between groups by weighting and combining, in a linear fashion, the variables that "best" distinguish the groups from each other. The S P S S discriminant function analysis program has two major features that are of importance here—an analysis feature that determines both the number and identity (by significant changes in Rao's V) of the variables in the total data set that contribute most to differentiating among the groups, and a classification feature that permits one to measure empirically the reliability of the discriminant functions by the proportion of correct classifications (Nie et al. 1975). Among the males, the first 30 variables were significant whereas, among the females, most of the discriminating information was contained in the first 28 variables.

Because of the inherent difficulties in visualizing the distances among these groups as measured by the discriminant function axes and group centroids in n-dimensional space, the final F values in the F matrices were converted to Mahalanobis' D^2 distances. The resulting D^2 matrices were keypunched for entry into the computer program DENDROGRAPH (McCammon and Wenniger 1970) as modified by David K. Taylor (personal communication). The final plot of the D^2 distances among the four sites (with males and females combined and including the 30 significant variables) is presented in figure 1. Based upon the magnitude of distance measured along both the vertical and horizontal axes, we must reject the null hypothesis that these four skeletal samples were obtained from a single biological population.

Test Situation No. 5: The multivariate approach employing 24 bilaterally scored discrete cranial traits and four medially scored discrete cranial traits was used to measure biological distance between the three Arkansas and the Kane Mounds samples.

Because of questions concerning the independence of discrete cranial traits, a total of 630 chi-square tests of independence were computed for the adult male and the adult female crania composing the total samples for each site. Of these, only six spurious correlations between sex and deformity were recorded (e.g., left frontal foramina were associated with deformed Hazel female crania).

Based upon the results of the preliminary analyses, these discrete cranial trait data were then entered into the MEAN MEASURE OF DIVERGENCE computer program for analysis. Four separate computer

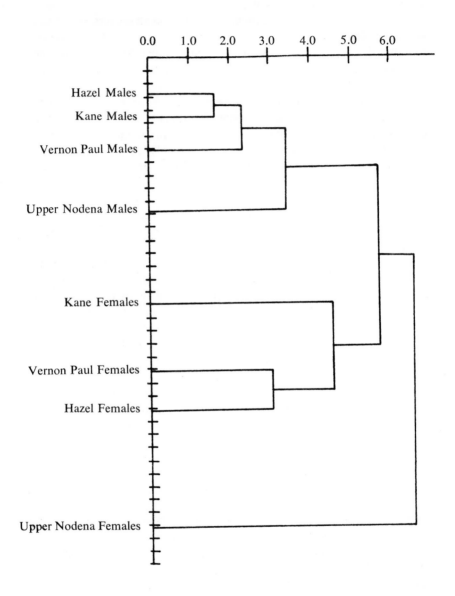

Figure 1. Biological Distance Between Samples
Measured by Mahalanobis' D² for 30 Variables and Both Sexes

analyses were performed employing the discrete trait data. In the first analysis, the controlling variables were site, sex, and bilateral traits scored by side. In the second analysis, the sexes were combined and the controlling variables were site and bilateral traits scored by side. The third analysis included the controlling variables of sex and site, but in this case the frequency of occurrence of the bilateral traits was analyzed by individuals. If the trait occurred on either or both sides, it was scored as present. In the fourth computer run, the controlling variables were site and the frequency of occurrence of traits in individuals with the sexes being pooled.

As in the case of the D^2 distance matrices, the significant θ^2 distances (Sjøvold 1973; Suchey 1975) for these various analyses were entered into the DENDROGRAPH program. The patterns that emerge are as follows: (1) the same general configurations occur irrespective of whether the traits were scored by side or by individual; (2) within sites, the sexes are closely related, indicating that they are members of the same gene pool (the discrepancy noted for the Vernon Paul males and females can be accounted for as sampling error due to the small sample sizes: see table 2); and (3) the distances between the samples are generally large, with Hazel and Upper Nodena being the most similar and the Kane and Vernon Paul samples being the most different from each other and from the Hazel and Upper Nodena samples. Based upon these results, the null hypothesis that these samples were drawn from a single population must again be rejected in favor of the alternate hypothesis. The results of the analyses (see figure 2) measuring distance for the single gene component are generally concordant with those measuring distance for the polygenic component.

SUMMARY AND CONCLUSIONS

The original goal of this study was to examine in detail, from a biological perspective, one of the several archeological interpretations proposed to account for the distribution of prehistoric Mississippian culture throughout the southeastern United States. Specifically, this research was designed to confirm or reject the hypothesis that Mississippian groups belonged to a single biological population.

In order to test the primary hypothesis that no significant genetic differences, as reflected in the skeletal phenotypes, would be observed among the various geographical groups represented by the Hazel, Vernon Paul, Upper Nodena, Kane, Dickson, and Irene samples, five test situations and subsidiary hypotheses were tested employing univariate and

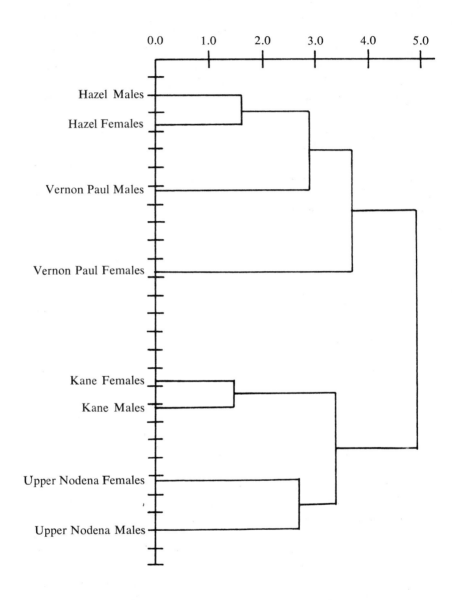

Figure 2. Biological Distance Between Samples Measured
by θ^2 for Discrete Traits Scored by Individual with Sexes Separated

multivariate techniques. In only one test situation, the univariate testing of the validity of pooling the three Arkansas samples, could the null hypothesis that no differences existed be accepted. The acceptance of this hypothesis was later refuted during the multivariate analyses of both the metric and discrete data from these sites. In all other tests, three univariate and two multivariate, the null hypothesis was rejected. It appears that the six samples were derived from at least four and, perhaps, six separate populations. In other words, the biological data fail to support the migration hypothesis.

Though modest indeed and far from being the definitive study in attempting to reconstruct the biological history of the prehistoric Mississippian peoples, this study has made a preliminary step in the investigation of the Mississippian phenomenon. These results will, it is hoped, stimulate interest in collecting additional data under more stringently controlled circumstances that would permit not only a retest of these conclusions, but also an in-depth examination of the other two archeological interpretations.

NOTES

1. The term *hypostotic* refers to the condition in which structures that are normally ossified in the skeleton have failed to do so. Such cases represent instances of arrested morphogenesis. *Hyperstotic* refers to the condition of excessive ossification—e.g., structures that would normally be soft tissues (cartilage, ligament, or dura) have ossified.

2. A phenocopy is an environmentally produced change in an organism (phenotype) that mimics a trait or condition normally produced by inheritance. For example, x-rays administered during the second or third month of pregnancy can produce microcephaly that is indistinguishable from the inherited form of microcephaly.

3. The term *os Inca* was employed by Rivero and Von Tschudi in 1853 to denote the condition in which the squamosal, or apical, portion of the occipital bone remains as a separate bone in the adult because the biasterionic suture has failed to close.

REFERENCES

Bang, G., and A. Hasund, 1972. Morphologic Characteristics of the Alaskan Eskimo: II. Carabelli's Cusp. *American Journal of Physical Anthropology* 37 : 35–40.

Bass, W. M., 1971. *Human Osteology: A Laboratory and Field Manual of the Human Skeleton* (Columbia: Missouri Archaeological Society).

Benfer, R. A., 1970. Associations among Cranial Traits. *American Journal of Physical Anthropology* 32 : 463–464.

Berry, A. C., 1974. The Use of Non-Metrical Variations of the Cranium in the Study of Scandinavian Population Movements. *American Journal of Physical Anthropology* 40 : 345–358.

Berry, A. C., and R. J. Berry, 1967. Epigenetic Variation in the Human Cranium. *Journal of Anatomy* 101 : 361–379.

Blakely, R. L., 1976. Biological Distance Between Late Woodland and Middle Mississippian Inhabitants of the Central Illinois River Valley. In *Approaches to the Study of Prehistory: A Bio-archaeological Perspective*, J. E. Buikstra, ed. (Evanston: Northwestern University Archaeological Program), in press.

Corruccini, R. S., 1974. An Examination of the Meaning of Cranial Discrete Traits for Human Skeletal Biological Studies. *American Journal of Physical Anthropology* 40 : 425–446.

———, 1976. The Interaction between Nonmetric and Metric Cranial Variation. *American Journal of Physical Anthropology* 44 : 285–294.

DeJarnette, D. L., 1952. Alabama Archeology: A Summary. In *Archeology of Eastern United States*, J. B. Griffin, ed. (Chicago: University of Chicago Press), pp. 272–284.

Diamond, M., 1952. *Dental Anatomy* (New York: Macmillan).

Fairbanks, C. H., 1952. Creek and Pre-Creek. In *Archeology of Eastern United States*, J. B. Griffin, ed. (Chicago: University of Chicago Press), pp. 285–300.

Gilbert, B. M., and T. W. McKern, 1973. A Method for Aging the Female *Os Pubis*. *American Journal of Physical Anthropology* 38 : 31–38.

Griffin, J. B., 1952. Culture Periods in Eastern United States Archeology. In *Archeology of Eastern United States*, J. B. Griffin, ed. (Chicago: University of Chicago Press), pp. 352–364.

———, 1967. Eastern North American Archaeology: A Summary. *Science* 156 : 175–191.

Harn, A. D., 1971. *The Prehistory of Dickson Mounds: A Preliminary Report*, Dickson Mounds Museum Anthropological Studies, No. 1 (Springfield: Illinois State Museum).

Hrdlička, A., 1908. Report on a Collection of Crania from Arkansas. *Journal of the Academy of Natural Science* 13 : 558–563.

———, 1909. Report on an Additional Collection of Skeletal Remains from Arkansas and Louisiana. *Journal of the Academy of Natural Science* 14 : 173–240.

Hulse, F. S., 1941. The People Who Lived at Irene. In *Irene Mound Site, Chatham County, Georgia*, by J. R. Caldwell and C. McCann (Athens: University of Georgia Press), pp. 57–68.

Jantz, R., 1973. Microevolutionary Change in Arikara Crania: A Multivariate Analysis. *American Journal of Physical Anthropology* 38 : 15–26.

Kellock, W. L., and P. A. Parsons, 1970. Variation of Minor Non-Metrical Skeletal Variants in Australian Aborigines. *American Journal of Physical Anthropology* 32 : 409–422.

Krogman, W. M., 1962. *The Human Skeleton in Forensic Medicine* (Springfield: Charles C Thomas).

Lane, R. A., 1969. *Population Perspective in Osteology: A Case Study* (M.A. thesis, Florida Atlantic University).

McCammon, R. B., and G. Wenniger, 1970. *The Dendrograph*, State Geological Survey, Computer Contributions No. 48 (Lawrence: University of Kansas Press).

McKern, T. W., and T. D. Stewart, 1957. *Skeletal Age Changes in Young American Males Analyzed from the Standpoint of Identification.* Headquarters Quartermaster Research and Development Command, Technical Report EP–45 (Natick, Mass.).

Melbye, F. J., 1963. *The Kane Burial Mounds* (Carbondale: Southern Illinois University Press).

Morse, D. F., 1973. *Nodena,* Arkansas Archeological Survey, Research Series No. 4 (Fayetteville: Arkansas Archeological Survey).

Neitzel, R. S., 1965. *Archaeology of the Fatherland Site: The Grand Village of the Natchez,* American Museum of Natural History, Anthropological Papers, Vol. 51, Part 1 (New York: American Museum of Natural History).

Neumann, G. K., 1937. Preliminary Notes on the Crania from Fulton County, Illinois. In *Rediscovering Illinois,* Fay-Cooper Cole and T. Deuel, eds. (Chicago: University of Chicago Press), pp. 227–264.

Newman, M. T., and C. E. Snow, 1942. Preliminary Report on the Skeletal Material from Pickwick Basin, Alabama. In *An Archeological Survey of Pickwick Basin in the Adjacent Portions of the States of Alabama, Mississippi, and Tennessee,* W. S. Webb and D. L. DeJarnette, eds., Smithsonian Institution, Bureau of American Ethnology, Bulletin 129 : 395–507.

Nie, N. H., C. Hadlai Hull, J. G. Jenkins, K. Steinbrenner, and D. H. Bent, 1975. *SPSS: Statistical Package for the Social Sciences* (New York: McGraw-Hill).

Ossenberg, N. S., 1969. *Discontinuous Morphological Variation in the Human Cranium* (Ph.D. diss., University of Toronto).

————, 1970. The Influence of Artificial Cranial Deformation on Discontinuous Morphological Traits. *American Journal of Physical Anthropology* 33 : 357–372.

Peebles, C. S., 1971. Moundville and Surrounding Sites: Some Structural Considerations of Mortuary Practices. In *Approaches to the Social Dimensions of Mortuary Practices,* J. A. Brown, ed. Memoirs of the Society for American Archaeology, No. 25, pp. 68–91.

Perino, G. H., 1971. The Mississippian Component at the Schild Site (No. 4), Greene County, Illinois. In *Mississippian Site Archaeology in Illinois: 1,* James A. Brown, ed., Illinois Archaeological Survey, Bulletin No. 8 (Urbana: University of Illinois Press), pp. 1–148.

Phenice, T. W., 1969. A Newly Developed Visual Method of Sexing the *Os Pubis. American Journal of Physical Anthropology* 30 : 297–302.

Quimby, G. I., 1942. The Natchezan Culture Type. *American Antiquity* 7 : 255–275.

Rightmire, G. P., 1972. Cranial Measurements and Discrete Traits Compared in Distance Studies of African Negro Skulls. *Human Biology* 44 : 263–276.

Rivero, M. E., and J. J. von Tschudi, 1853. *Antiquities Peruviennes* (Os Inca), F. L. Hawks, trans. (Cincinnati: A. S. Barnes).

Schour, I., and M. Massler, 1941. The Development of the Human Dentition. *Journal of the American Dental Association* 28 : 1153–1160.

Sjøvold, T., 1973. The Occurrence of Minor Non-Metrical Variation in the Skeleton and Their Quantitative Treatment for Population Comparisons. *Homo* 24 : 204–233.

Suchey, J. M., 1975. *Biological Distances of Prehistoric California Populations Derived from Non-Metric Traits of the Cranium* (Ph.D. diss., University of California, Riverside).

Wolf, D. J., 1976. *A Population Model for the Analysis of Osteological Materials* (Ph.D. diss., University of Arizona).

Sociocultural Implications of Demographic Data from Etowah, Georgia

Robert L. Blakely

Archeology has yet to benefit fully from the methods and theories of demography. Biological anthropologists, who have been in a position to collect demographic data from skeletal populations, may be more responsible for this gap than are archeologists, who stand to gain the most from demographic investigations. Biological anthropologists, because of traditional concerns with racial typology and evolutionary morphology, have failed to provide information that could help archeologists answer questions about human adaptations. The revealing works of Vallois (1960), Laughlin (1968), Acsádi and Nemeskéri (1970), Buikstra (1972), Coale (1972), Weiss (1972 and 1973), and Peebles (1974) have resulted in the recognition by biological anthropologists and archeologists alike of the potential value of demographic studies in the interpretation of cultural processes.

The present study compares data collected from two skeletal samples, Mound C and village area series, at Etowah, Georgia, in order to reconstruct partially the health environment of the populations and to suggest mechanisms of sociocultural adaptation. Mortality profiles of both samples are constructed to illustrate fluctuations in the relative frequencies of deaths occurring within all age groups. The paper argues that for the village sample the modes of the curve, which represent greatest numbers of deaths, reflect differential stress factors, both physical and behavioral, operating at certain ages. In contrast, because the Mound C profile is not age stable (see below), the peaks cannot be interpreted demographically and, therefore, sociocultural phenomena are implicated. The study brings multivariate discriminant analysis of the Etowah samples, using craniometric data, to bear on questions pertaining to societal structure. All of the information is then employed to suggest adaptive and maladaptive elements of the mature Mississippian culture in northern Georgia.

The Etowah site is situated on the floodplain of the Etowah River as it winds westward through the Piedmont section of northwest Georgia.

It was occupied intermittently by Mississippian Indians from roughly A.D. 1040 until early in the historic period (Crane and Griffin 1959). The location of Etowah allowed its inhabitants to exploit three diverse ecological zones—Piedmont, Great Valley, and Appalachian Plateau— as well as to utilize the rich alluvial valley soil for agriculture (Larson 1971).[1] Larson (1971) also points out that the site's location adjacent to different ecological zones meets one of the conditions necessary for the development of a stratified redistributional society (Service 1962).

Etowah is probably best known for the elaborate paraphernalia associated with the burials interred in Mound C and ascribed to the "Southeastern Ceremonial Complex" or "Southern Cult" (Waring and Holder 1945). From the work of Kelly and Larson, much has been learned about the chronology of the site and the social organization of the people who built the mounds (Kelly and Larson 1957; Larson 1959, 1971, and 1972).

Less is known about the people buried in the village area east of Mound A (fig. 1). The individuals interred in this area and the intrusive burials in Mound B, later in time than the Mound C interments, date primarily from the late prehistoric and early historic periods and do not usually possess the finely made grave goods associated with the earlier burials.

Larson (1971) is convinced that the superordinate (Mound C) group had exclusive control over exotic materials, which served to demonstrably delineate and reinforce the dual social stratification.[2] It is, in part, the differential quality and distribution of artifacts that leads Larson (1971) to conclude that social status was ascriptive rather than achieved and that there may have been ascribed statuses within the superordinate segment based on descent groups.

The model invoked, then, is that of a chiefdom model of social organization. Presumably, the criteria for proposing a chiefdom at Etowah are the following: (1) specific symbols of rank and office, (2) presence of richly adorned infant burials among Mound C interments, (3) apparent energy expended in selective mortuary ceremonialism, (4) evidence for organized productive activities that transcend household duties, and (5) probable existence of a redistributional society, although Peebles (n.d.) contends that this is not a necessary requirement for a chiefdom. These criteria are predicated on a crucial, and probably valid, assumption that links burials with social organization: ". . . that individuals who are treated differentially in life will also be treated differentially in death" (Peebles 1974 : 38).

The demographic data to follow support the idea that Etowah represented a socially stratified society, but they do not support the argument

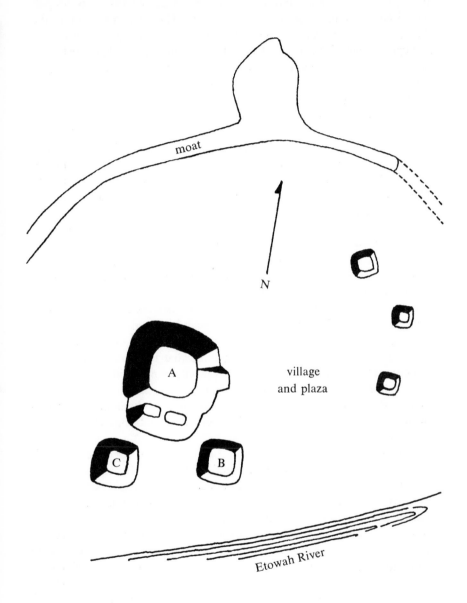

Figure 1. Mound C and the village area at the Etowah
site in Bartow County, Georgia (adapted from Larson 1971).

for a predominantly ascriptive society. They suggest instead that status was more commonly achieved than ascribed. The implication is that the society at Etowah was more complex than that of either a chiefdom or an egalitarian society, but rather contained a more flexible, adaptive social structure that combined elements of both.

MATERIALS AND METHODS

Before one attempts to interpret information obtained from skeletal samples, one must be sure that the samples meet several criteria and that the populations are large enough to constitute statistically valid samples. The Etowah village sample consists of 76 individuals, and the Mound C sample consists of 171 individuals. Both of these, according to Weiss (1973), are of sufficient size to justify their use if another demographic criterion is met. Demographic theory requires that populations be stable; that is, they must be of infinite size, have no net immigration or outmigration, and have fixed rates of fertility and mortality at each age (Weiss 1973). While it is theoretically possible to ascertain stability in living populations, it is virtually impossible to do so in skeletal series. However, Weiss (1973) reported that if the adult mortality curve approximates a pyramid, that is, shows more deaths during the middle range of the potential life span, one can assume that the sample approaches stability. The Etowah village mortality profile is pyramidal, so the population is a validly constituted sample (see fig. 2). This profile further means that unlike some Hopewell and other Mississippian groups (Blakely 1971), separate cemeteries were not established for different age groups.

The mortality curve of the Mound C sample, on the other hand, is bimodal and evidences few infant and child deaths. Because it violates the age-stable criterion, nondemographic factors (that is, sociocultural patterns) must be sought to explain why certain individuals were included and others excluded from Mound C interment.

It is important to note that since all of the people that make up the Etowah populations are dead, the skeletal samples (and any other skeletal series) are by definition pathological. The tendency on the part of the investigator, then, is to view the health environment as a relatively bad one unless he or she recognizes that the conditions that led to death were not necessarily similar to those that contributed to life. It is obvious, however, that in order to explore prehistory, the biological anthropologist has no recourse other than to utilize skeletons.

The validity of the interpretation of demographic data also depends

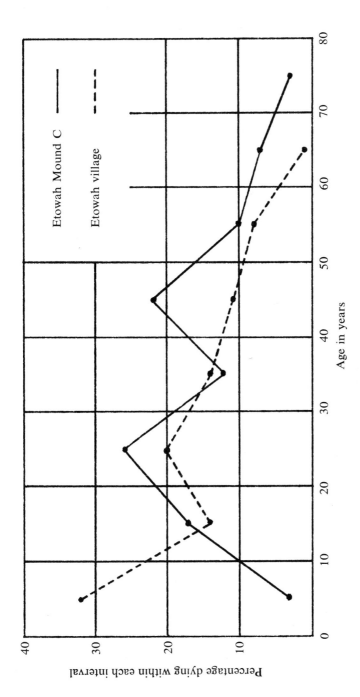

Figure 2. Mortality profiles of the Mound C skeletal sample (sexes combined, N=171) and village skeletal sample (sexes combined, N=76).

on the ability of the researcher to determine age and sex accurately. It is equally important neither to consistently skew ages toward one end of the age continuum, nor to systematically bias sex assignment, a frequent albeit unintentional practice among both inexperienced and experienced investigators (Weiss 1972). Sexual dimorphism in the Etowah village and Mound C samples was great enough to insure accurate identification of the sex of adults. Of the 52 adults and adolescents in the village population, 26 were designated male and 26 female. In the Mound C sample, 94 were assigned male and 71 female; a chi-square test indicated that these frequencies do not deviate significantly from the expected 1 : 1 ratio. Because there exist no adequate criteria for distinguishing subadolescent males and females, no attempt was made to separate the sexes of infants and children.

A brief description of the criteria employed to determine skeletal age at death should serve to document the validity of my methodology. Multiple criteria were applied discriminantly whenever possible to obtain maximum accuracy. Subadolescents (neonate to twelve years) were assigned ages on the basis of calcification and eruption of deciduous and permanent dentition (Dahlberg 1963), linear length of long bones (Bass 1971), and ossification and fusion of bony elements such as the neural arches of the vertebrae (Bass 1971). It is generally assumed that these age indicators substantiate each other, and they usually do; but in some instances contradictory evidence makes age assessment somewhat more difficult. In these cases, dental development and eruption were regarded as the most reliable criteria of skeletal age (Johnston 1969).

The ages of adolescents (12–20 years) were determined primarily from epiphyseal union of long bones, taking into account sex differences in the rate of maturation (Stewart and Trotter 1954). According to Krogman (1962), the pubic symphysis is the most reliable age indicator beyond nineteen years. In this study, age changes in the symphyseal face (McKern and Stewart 1957) were considered to provide the most accurate and consistent measures of age and were relied upon when discrepancies arose. Epiphyseal union up to age twenty-eight (Stewart and Trotter 1954), dental attrition (Brothwell 1965), and endocranial suture closure (Todd and Lyon 1925), when corroborated by other criteria or the only available evidence, were employed in addition to determine the ages of individuals beyond twenty years.

The method of developing the information to provide a demographic profile of the Etowah village population is illustrated in table 1. Mortality profiles, it should be noted, can be constructed in a number of ways, so that by modifying the age intervals one is able to change slightly the shape of the curve to meet the objectives of the investigator. It is possible, in selecting to group individuals in ten-year intervals, to show gross fluctuations in mortality, which may have masked smaller but potentially significant modes within the intervals. In this project, however, given the vagaries of age assessment, particularly of individuals of advanced age, it seemed inadvisable to attempt a further breakdown of age categories.

The mortality rate, according to Weiss (1973), can be calculated by dividing the number of specimens in each age category by the total number of specimens surviving until the onset of that particular decade (see table 1). Thus, in the 50–59 age group, the six deaths were divided by the seven individuals in the sample who were not dead by age fifty, yielding a mortality rate of .857. The mortality rate, then, represents the probability of dying during any given age interval. While this is a handy mathematical means for expressing the likelihood of death—an important demographic parameter—it was felt that the mortality rate does not reflect the periods of life and death crises that were recognized by the Etowah people. That opinion is based on the fact that the ethnographic evidence from many contemporary societies indicates that deaths among comparatively young individuals are more poorly received than deaths among the elderly (Driver 1961). The absolute frequencies or the percentages of deaths, therefore, may be more sensitive indicators of the peoples' apprehension over certain age crises. Survivorship rate is simply the reciprocal of the mortality rate, expressing the likelihood of making it through any particular decade.

The relative frequencies and percentages of individuals in age groups

Table 1.
Frequencies and Percentages of Deaths, Mortality Rates,
and Survivorship Rates within Ten-Year Intervals
for the Etowah Village Sample (sexes combined, $N = 76$)

Age Interval	Frequency	Cumulative Frequency	Percentage	Cumulative Percentage	Mortality Rate	Survivorship Rate
0–9	24	24	32	32	.315	.685
10–19	11	35	14	46	.212	.788
20–29	15	50	20	66	.366	.634
30–39	11	61	14	80	.423	.577
40–49	8	69	11	91	.533	.467
50–59	6	75	8	99	.857	.143
60–69	1	76	1	100	1.000	.000
70–79	0	76	0	100	—	—

Table 2.
Frequencies and Percentages of Deaths, Mortality Rates,
and Survivorship Rates within Ten-Year Intervals
for the Etowah Mound C Sample (sexes combined, $N = 171$).

Age Interval	Frequency	Cumulative Frequency	Percentage	Cumulative Percentage	Mortality Rate	Survivorship Rate
0–9	6	6	3	3	.035	.965
10–19	29	35	17	20	.176	.824
20–29	43	78	26	46	.316	.684
30–39	21	99	12	58	.226	.774
40–49	37	136	22	80	.514	.486
50–59	17	153	10	90	.486	.514
60–69	12	165	7	97	.667	.333
70–79	6	171	3	100	1.000	.000

represented in Mound C are displayed in table 2. Because the sample is not age stable, mortality rate and survivorship rate cannot be considered to have the same meanings that they did in the village sample (table 1). Mortality and survivorship rates of Mound C interments represent, respectively, the likelihood for inclusion and exclusion of individuals in any given age category. The probability for inclusion in Mound C is thus greatest after forty years and least likely before ten years.

RESULTS

Etowah village mortality percentages in age intervals are graphically represented in figure 2 and compared with those of the Mound C sample. While the Mound C curve differs dramatically from those of other prehistoric populations in the eastern United States, the village profile is very similar to the curves of other Mississippian groups. General measures of mortality support the latter finding. The average age at death for the Etowah village population is twenty-three years compared with twenty-four years among Illinois (Dickson Mounds) Mississippians (Blakely 1971). By age ten years, almost one-third (32 percent) of the Etowah village people had died (35 percent for Illinois Mississippians). Of the village population 91 percent had died by age fifty years (89 percent among Illinois Mississippians). At the Etowah village, the youngest deaths occurred among prematurely born neonates and the oldest member was a female over sixty years. I have argued elsewhere (Blakely and Mathews 1975) that the similar figures and mortality curves suggest that the health environments of these two Mississippian groups were comparable.

Because of the rapid rate of maturation among infants and children, it is possible to determine more precisely the ages of subadolescents, permitting the identification of fluctuations within the initial ten-year interval. At the Etowah village, 10 percent of the entire population died during the first year after birth. This figure, which is not unusual for prehistoric Americans, is high when compared with those from modern, technologically developed societies—about 2 percent in the United States in 1970 (Freedman and Berelson 1974). The mortality rate certainly reflects a comparative lack of knowledge and technology concerning childbirth and early health care.[3]

The next significant rise in the curve of the village sample occurs between the second and third decade; it is illustrated by separate histograms of male and female mortality in figure 3. Male deaths increased from 18 percent in the second decade to 24 percent in the third decade, while female mortality rose from 11 percent to 20 percent. The increased number of female deaths is probably attributable to the deleterious consequences of childbearing, a maladaptive aspect of life shared by many early populations.[4] What is more puzzling is the larger number of male fatalities throughout the teens and twenties. Warfare and hunting activities seem to offer the only explanations, although the skeletons fail to substantiate that possibility, there being few identifiable incidences of accidental or purposefully inflicted injuries among males in these age groups. Although Hernando De Soto is thought to have explored the Etowah Valley during the time of village occupation (Bourne 1904), no evidence was found that European diseases affected mortality (Blakely and Mathews 1975). It should be pointed out, however, that diseases such as mumps, measles, and smallpox are rarely manifested on bones.

The declining curve in the forties, fifties, and sixties poses no mystery. Fewer people were dying throughout these later years, not because they were less likely to die, but because there were fewer of them left to die. The probability of dying in the forties was over 50 percent and the figure rises to over 80 percent in the fifties (table 1). These fatalities can be attributed primarily to so-called old age diseases.

In examining the Mound C mortality profile (fig. 2), one is struck by the disparate percentages of deaths between Etowah village and Mound C samples, particularly during the first, third, and fifth decades. A chi-square test of the likelihood that the differential frequencies in three age

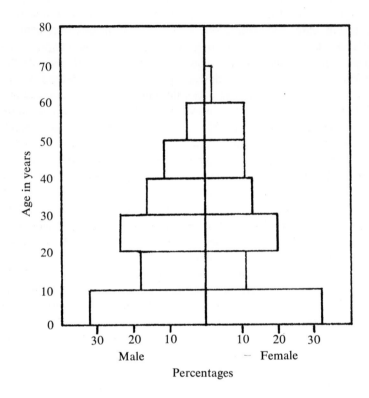

Figure 3. Percentages of males and females dying within ten-year intervals for the village sample. (Proportions are based on 100% for each sex; subadolescent percentages assume equal numbers of male and female deaths.)

categories could be due to chance is displayed in table 3. Because the probability is 0.001, one must seek explanations for the discrepancies.

Particularly intriguing is the fact that only 3 percent of the Mound C interments were under age ten years. This figure contrasts to the 32 percent mortality rate in the village and is well below first-decade mortality in the United States in 1970 (Freedman and Berelson 1974). It is possible, of course, that those destined for interment in Mound C received special health care, but unless one assumes that health treatment of Mound C Mississippians was over twice as efficacious as that provided in modern United States hospitals, one is forced to conclude that infants and children were selectively excluded from interment in Mound C.

The two modes in the Mound C profile, one consisting of individuals in their twenties and the other of individuals in their forties, are interesting because of their sex composition. The histograms in figure 4 show that over 70 percent of the burials comprising the mode in the third decade are females. Conversely, the large majority of the burials included in the fifth decade are males. As a result of age differences between female and male inclusions in Mound C, the average age at death for Mound C females is thirty years and that of Mound C males is forty years. In table 4, a chi-square test of the disparate frequencies of males and females in three age categories indicates that the differences are statistically significant at the 0.001 level of probability.

A last mortality comparison between Etowah village and Mound C males (table 5) shows opposing tendencies. In the village, the numbers of deaths decrease as age increases. On the other hand, among Mound C males, the likelihood for inclusion increases with advancing age (11 percent below age sixteen years, 29 percent for ages sixteen to thirty-

Table 3.
Three-by-Two Contingency Table
Illustrating Differential Frequencies and Percentages of Deaths
in Three Age Groups Between All Village and Mound C Individuals.*

Age Group (years)	Village		Mound C	
	Freq.	%	Freq.	%
0–15	29	38	20	12
16–35	28	37	73	43
36+	19	25	78	45

* Chi-square (χ^2) and probability (p, two degrees of freedom) predict the likelihood that the differences are due to chance. $\chi^2 = 24.590$; $p < 0.001$.

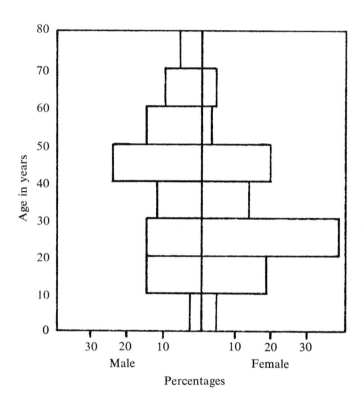

Figure 4. Percentages of males and females dying within ten-year intervals for the Mound C sample. (Proportions are based on 100% for each sex; subadolescent percentages assume equal numbers of male and female deaths.)

Table 4.
Three-by-Two Contingency Table
Illustrating Differential Frequencies and Percentages of Deaths
in Three Age Groups between Mound C Males and Females.*

Age Group (years)	Mound C Males		Mound C Females	
	Freq.	%	Freq.	%
0–15	11	11	9	12
16–35	28	29	45	61
36+	58	60	20	27

* Chi-square (χ^2) and probability (p, two degrees of freedom) predict the likelihood that the differences are due to chance. $\chi^2 = 19.980$; $p < 0.001$.

five years, and 60 percent beyond age thirty-five years). The frequencies from which these percentages were derived are significantly different at the 0.001 level.

It might be tempting to explain the Mound C "male mode" and "female mode" in the ways suggested for their village counterparts: that is, warfare and hunting for males and childbearing for females. These alternatives appear untenable, however, in light of the high social status and probable preferential treatment enjoyed by Mound C individuals. Why, for example, should almost 40 percent of the Mound C females die during the third decade when only 20 percent of the village females died throughout the same period? The advanced age and high status of most

Table 5.
Three-by-Two Contingency Table
Illustrating Differential Frequencies and Percentages of Deaths
in Three Age Groups between Village Males and Mound C Males.*

Age Group (years)	Village Males		Mound C Males	
	Freq.	%	Freq.	%
0–15	16	42	11	11
16–35	13	34	28	29
36+	9	24	58	60

* Chi-square (χ^2) and probability (p, two degrees of freedom) predict the likelihood that the differences are due to chance. $\chi^2 = 20.415$; $p < 0.001$.

Mound C males makes it unlikely that they would be dying from injuries resulting from warfare and hunting.

Sociocultural implications of these demographic data from Etowah are several. First, because Mound C was the burial site of high-status individuals, and infants and children were virtually excluded from interment in the mound, and inclusion in Mound C was significantly correlated with the advancing ages of males, it therefore seems probable that high status among males was achieved, not ascribed. Females included in Mound C are generally younger than the males, indicating that they achieved high status at an earlier age. One can conclude that they were apparently deriving their status through marriage to high-status males who were, therefore, probably older. Over 50 percent of the females interred in Mound C were under thirty years old, indicating that it is at least possible that wives were frequently sacrificed upon the deaths of their husbands, as Sears (1956) has suggested was the case at the Mississippian site of Kolomoki in southwestern Georgia. Little evidence of sacrifice was found on the female skeletons in Mound C, but many techniques for sacrifice would leave no marks on bones, and I did discover conclusive evidence that sacrifice was practiced at Etowah. The fact that six richly accompanied subadolescent burials were among the 171 Mound C burials studied may mean that the status of the single, most powerful ("Eagle Warrior") family was inherited and not earned.

In light of these possibilities, it became important to conduct a test of biological similarities and differences between Etowah village and Mound C populations. The assumption was that if the samples were shown to be statistically indistinguishable, that would lend credence to the conclusions above. It would demonstrate that the members of both groups emerged from the same breeding population rather than from genetically isolated groups. On the other hand, if the samples proved to be dissimilar, the differences could be attributed to genotypic changes resulting from the division of ranks, or variances in phenotypic expressions due to differential care and treatment, or both.

Multivariate analysis of four Etowah subsamples—village females, village males, Mound C males, and Mound C females—was undertaken using the Biomed Stepwise Discriminant Analysis (BMD07M) computer program (Dixon 1971) to test for the biological relatedness of the Etowah samples.[5] Subadults were omitted from this comparison because their inclusion would have artificially reduced populational differences (Blakely 1973).[6] From a data bank of over one hundred cranial and postcranial measurements and indices, a subset of sixteen craniometric variables was ultimately settled upon for multivariate comparison;[7] the subset was chosen primarily because these continuous cranial attributes have been shown to be the least affected by artificial cranial deformation, a cultural practice commonly evidenced on the skulls of males and females in both Etowah samples, and because these particular osteometric variables provided the most complete data (i.e., were least subject to fragmentation and loss occasioned by poor preservation).[8]

The biological distances between the four subsamples and the relative morphological positions of all individuals comprising the subsamples are illustrated in figure 5. The groups appear to be separated out, but this dispersion is deceiving because the greatest distance between any two samples is between Mound C females and Mound C males, a distinction apparently based on sexual dimorphism rather than populational dissimilarities. Tables 6 and 7 provide information for interpreting the data presented in figure 5. Table 6 lists the biological distances (Jantz 1972) between each of the samples.[9] Notice that the next to least distance is between village males and Mound C males. Table 7 illustrates that none of the distances between Etowah subsamples are statistically significant even using the highest tolerance level of 0.05.

Thus, the multivariate test indicates that the Etowah village and Mound C populations are statistically inseparable on the basis of craniometric morphology. This, in turn, is yet another piece of evidence favoring the hypothesis that in earning one's status, one also resolved whether burial would be in Mound C or elsewhere.

SUMMARY AND DISCUSSION

The mortality profile of the village population showed that the health environment of the Etowah people was not unlike that of the Illinois Mississippians and probably was comparable to similarly sized Mississippian groups throughout the eastern United States. It becomes a reasonable

Table 6.
D (biological distance) Values Between Village Females,
Village Males, Mound C Males, and Mound C Females.

	Village Females	Village Males	Mound C Males
Village Males	4.31		
Mound C Males	6.30	4.36	
Mound C Females	6.95	5.44	7.26

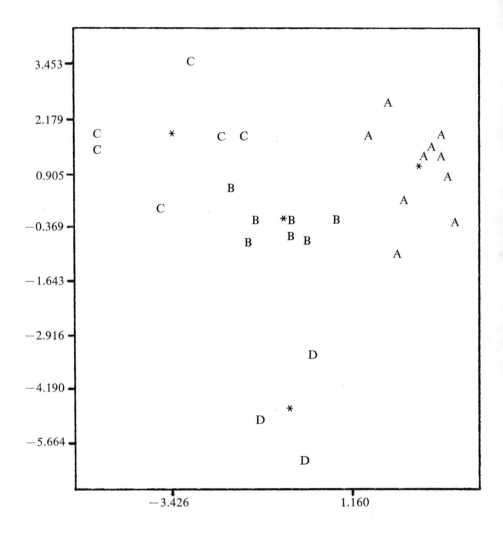

Figure 5. Group centroids (*) and distribution of village females (A), village males (B), Mound C males (C), and Mound C females (D) on canonical variables I, II, and III according to multivariate discriminant analysis using sixteen craniometric variables.

Table 7.
Final Matrix of F Statistics Between Village Females, Village Males, Mound C Males, and Mound C Females.

	Village Females	Village Males	Mound C Males
Village Males	1.52181*		
Mound C Males	2.96446*	1.22156*	
Mound C Females	2.08955*	1.23796*	2.09701*

degrees of freedom = 16,7.
* Not significant; $p > 0.05$.

conclusion given the facts that most large populations occupied riverine, woodland environments at roughly the same time, practiced maize horticulture supplemented by animal and wild plant foodstuffs, possessed similar levels of technology, and had roughly comparable population densities.

Ages at which death was more likely to occur among the Etowah Indians included birth, the twenties, and throughout the later years for both sexes. Times of relative security were during middle and late childhood and adolescence. Compared to the Illinois Mississippians, Etowah appears to have been a safer environment for neonates, weaning infants, and perhaps females in general, but a more dangerous environment for young males. No evidence was found that European diseases affected mortality at the Etowah village.

The mortality profile of the Mound C population cannot be interpreted demographically because it is not age-stable and that fact initially suggested that the curve's shape is a result of sociocultural phenomena. It was shown that infants and children were, by and large, excluded from interment in Mound C; the dearth of subadolescents is not likely due to superior health treatment, because that would require far better medical technology than that practiced in modern western society. The probability of male inclusion increases with advancing age (table 5), peaking among individuals in their forties. By contrast, the majority of female inclusions are under age thirty years. Remembering that Mound C was the location for the interments of high-status individuals in a stratified society, it appears that high status among males was achieved. It is further argued, because of the disparate age breakdowns of males and females included in Mound C, that females derived their status through marriage. Logic leads to the conclusion that many females were sacrificed at the death of their husbands. Although some societies resolve widow's status through kinship ties (Driver 1961), this may not have been feasible at Etowah because of the dual social structure. By sacrificing these females, they retained in death what their deceased mates could no longer provide. The same fate would not have awaited the offspring of the dead because their status had yet to be attained. Coupled with the recently recovered evidence for sacrifice among Mound C interments, this idea becomes a real possibility.[10] The presence of six richly accompanied subadolescents among Mound C burials suggests the possibility that the position of one family of absolute rulers was inherited.

One of the requirements for meeting the chiefdom model of social organization is that there be a well-defined dimension of ascribed ranking. Furthermore, as Peebles (1974) and others have pointed out, this ascribed dimension must include a partial ordering based on symbols, energy expenditure, and other variables of mortuary ritual, and that it cannot be simultaneously ordered on the bases of age and sex. Because Mound C interments violate the latter prerequisite, Etowah cannot be considered to conform completely to the chiefdom model. It does, nevertheless, evidence some attributes of a chiefdom.

Social organization at Etowah appears to include combined elements of both chiefdom and egalitarian societies. That Etowah does not fall entirely within one organizational scheme should not be of concern. There are, in fact, advantages to be gained by adopting multiple systems. By integrating aspects of more than one social structure, it is possible that the Etowah people made their society more flexible and thereby more adaptive, while at the same time maintaining organizational (hierarchical) efficiency.

Anthropologists may be deceiving, or at least limiting, themselves if they impose their existing conceptual models on all diverse societies. This is not to imply that models are unimportant; they are important because they serve as conceptual tools through which hypotheses can be generated, against which we test our data. These conclusions regarding Etowah social structure would not have been possible without using the chiefdom model, which was compared with the model constructed from the Etowah data. I am arguing that anthropologists not abuse this tool— that instead of trying to fit societies into models, anthropologists should adapt models to societies. When models are mistaken for reality, we have obviated the need for the models.

Comparative demographic and biological information as has been provided in this study can, if properly applied, add a new and important dimension to archeological inquiry. In addition, this study demonstrates the need for an integrative, systematic approach to anthropological research. Only when archeologists, biological anthropologists, and other investigators cooperate will truly meaningful statements emerge about prehistoric cultural processes.[11]

NOTES

1. Larson (1972) contends that competition for fertile bottomlands led to endemic warfare in the Southeast; his evidence rests primarily on the presence of fortified villages, expansive population (indicated by successive enlargement of palisaded enclosures), and high correlation between arable soils and Mississippian villages. Gibson (1974) advanced an alternative, but not necessarily contradictory, hypothesis that sporadic fighting served as a principal equilibrium-regulating institution among ranked societies.

2. Because the Mound C interments and most of the village area burials are not contemporaneous, they cannot be cited as direct evidence of a dually ranked society. That fact does not, however, detract from Larson's argument that there was social stratification at Etowah during the Wilbanks (mound- and plaza-building) period.

3. Among many Old and New World populations, a small rise in mortality is also observed around ages two and three years (Angel 1969). Often individuals comprising this mode evidence bony lesions indicative of porotic hyperostosis, a condition usually attributable to either dietary deficiencies or anemias (Blakely 1971). I have hypothesized that these fatalities among Mississippian Indians may be due to malnutrition brought about by unsuccessful weaning, a failure on the part of the infant to make successfully the transition from a lactiferous to a hard diet (Blakely 1971). This mode is not apparent in the Etowah sample, suggesting that they somehow circumvented this potentially dangerous occurrence.

4. An alternative explanation is that if male fatalities were incurred away from home and if these individuals were not brought back to the cemetery for interment, a comparable ratio of male-to-female deaths might be observed. This seems unlikely, however, given the equal numbers of males and females in the total sample.

5. Space does not permit full discussion of the usefulness and validity of multivariate techniques for the study of human biological affinities. Suffice it to cite some references and a quote from Howells (1972) on the advantages of multivariate analysis. "Multivariate statistics . . . are . . . the natural and appropriate treatment of populations as such, or of several populations at once. Methodologically, they are the quantitative expression of 'population thinking' (Mayr 1959), and the corrective, in structuring hypotheses, for 'typological thinking' " (Howells 1972 : 127). For specific references on the multivariate approach taken herein, see Dixon (1971) and Blakely (1973 and 1976). For more general information on the use of multivariate statistics, consult Rao (1952), Cooley and Lohnes (1962), Howells and Crichton (1966), and Blackith and Reyment (1971).

6. Immature skeletons from any population sample, because morphology is incompletely developed, tend to resemble one another more than their adult counterparts and, therefore, must be excluded from all intergroup comparisons except those examining developmental changes.

7. The subset of measurements and indices consisted of the following: minimum frontal breadth, internal biorbital breadth, subtense to internal biorbital breadth, anterior interorbital breadth, left orbital breadth (maxillofrontale), left orbital breadth (dacryon), left orbital height, dacryal chord, subtense to dacryal chord, minimum nasal breadth, subtense to minimum nasal breadth, zygomatic height, facial flatness index, left orbital index (maxillofrontale), nasal root height index, and nasal bone height index.

8. This was an important procedural consideration because the computer program employed in the analysis required complete data for each individual in the samples, thus necessitating that a means be found to fill missing data without distorting the mean values of the metric data on which the multivariate comparison is predicated. Blakely and Mathews (1976) have found that when less than 10 percent of the data is missing, mean values of the existing data can be substituted for missing measurements without much distortion of the real figures; however, when 10 percent or more of the data is unavailable, regression formulae predict missing values more accurately. Because in the present study less than 10 percent of the measurements were unavailable, substituted means were employed.

9. Biological distance is the square root of the Mahalanobis' D^2, or generalized distance, statistic. D^2 can be calculated by summing the squared differences between the canonical variables evaluated at group means for the appropriate two samples.

10. Mortuary practices at Etowah may have been similar to those at Kolomoki, a Mississippian center in southwestern Georgia (Sears 1956). Mortuary ceremonialism in common at the two sites included burial in mounds, reburial in mounds, erection of a platform for mortuary rites, retainer sacrifice, and wife sacrifice. Sears (1956) draws parallels between Kolomoki burial ceremonies and Natchez mortuary practices. To learn whether Etowah mortuary ceremonialism compares with that of the Natchez will require further investigation.

11. This research was supported, in part, by National Science Foundation grant SOC–7503833. Thanks are due Roy S. Dickens, Jr., for his informative suggestions and critical reading of this manuscript.

REFERENCES

Acsádi, G., and J. Nemeskéri, 1970. *History of Human Life Span and Mortality* (Budapest: Akadémiai Kiadó).

Angel, J. L., 1969. Paleodemography and Evolution. *American Journal of Physical Anthropology* 31:343–353.

Bass, W. M., 1971. *Human Osteology: A Laboratory and Field Manual of the Human Skeleton* (Columbia: Missouri Archaeological Society).

Blackith, R. E., and R. A. Reyment, 1971. *Multivariate Morphometrics* (New York: Academic Press).

Blakely, R. L., 1971. Comparison of the Mortality Profiles of Archaic, Middle Woodland, and Middle Mississippian Skeletal Populations. *American Journal of Physical Anthropology* 34:43–54.

———, 1973. *Biological Variation Among and Between Two Prehistoric*

Indian Populations at Dickson Mounds (Ph.D. diss., Indiana University).
————, 1976. Biological Distance Between Late Woodland and Middle Mississippian Inhabitants of the Central Illinois River Valley. In *Approaches to the Study of Prehistory: A Bio-archaeological Perspective*, J. E. Buikstra, ed. (Evanston: Northwestern University Archaeological Program), in press.

Blakely, R. L., and D. S. Mathews, 1975. Demographic Model of the Etowah Village Population. *Bulletin of the Georgia Academy of Science* 33:168–179.

————, 1976. A Test of Missing Data Replacement Techniques in Multivariate Analysis of Skeletal Populations. (Paper presented at the 11th annual meeting of the Southern Anthropological Society, Atlanta.)

Bourne, E. G., 1904. *Narratives of the Career of Hernando de Soto,* vols. I and II (New York: A. S. Barnes).

Brothwell, D. R., 1965. *Digging Up Bones* (London: British Museum of Natural History).

Buikstra, J. E., 1972. *Hopewell in the Lower Illinois River Valley: A Regional Approach to the Study of Biological Variability and Mortuary Activity* (Ph.D. diss., University of Chicago).

Coale, A. J., 1972. *The Growth and Structure of Human Populations: A Mathematical Investigation* (Princeton: Princeton University Press).

Cooley, W. W., and P. R. Lohnes, 1962. *Multivariate Procedures for the Behavioral Sciences* (New York: John Wiley).

Crane, H. R., and J. B. Griffin, 1959. University of Michigan Radiocarbon Dates IV. *Radiocarbon Supplement* 1:173–198.

Dahlberg, A. A., 1963. Analysis of American Indian Dentition. In *Dental Anthropology*, D. R. Brothwell, ed. (New York: Pergamon Press), pp. 149–177.

Dixon, W. J., 1971. Biomedical Computer Programs. *University of California Publications in Automatic Computation*, No. 2 (Berkeley: University of California Press).

Driver, H. E., 1961. *Indians of North America* (Chicago: University of Chicago Press).

Freedman, R., and B. Berelson, 1974. The Human Population. *Scientific American* 231:31–39.

Gibson, J. L., 1974. Aboriginal Warfare in the Protohistoric Southeast: An Alternative Perspective. *American Antiquity* 39:130–133.

Howells, W. W., 1972. Analysis of Patterns of Variation in the Crania of Recent Man. In *The Functional and Evolutionary Biology of the Primates*, R. Tuttle, ed. (Chicago: Aldine), pp. 123–151.

Howells, W. W., and J. M. Crichton, 1966. Craniometry and Multivariate Analysis. *Papers of the Peabody Museum* 57:1–67.

Jantz, R. L., 1972. Cranial Variation and Microevolution in Arikara Skeletal Populations. *Plains Anthropologist* 17:20–35.

Johnston, F. E., 1969. Approaches to the Study of Developmental Variability in Human Skeletal Populations. *American Journal of Physical Anthropology* 31:335–341.

Kelly, A. R., and L. H. Larson, Jr., 1957. Explorations at Etowah, Georgia, 1954–1956. *Archaeology* 10:39–48.

Krogman, W. M., 1962. *The Human Skeleton in Forensic Medicine* (Springfield: Charles C Thomas).

Larson, L. H., Jr., 1959. A Mississippian Headdress from Etowah, Georgia. *American Antiquity* 25:109–112.

———, 1971. Archaeological Implications of Social Stratification at the Etowah Site, Georgia. In *Approaches to the Social Dimensions of Mortuary Practices*, J. A. Brown, ed. Memoirs of the Society for American Archaeology No. 25, pp. 58–67.

———, 1972. Functional Considerations of Warfare in the Southeast during the Mississippi Period. *American Antiquity* 37:383–392.

Laughlin, W. S., 1968. The Demography of Hunters: An Eskimo Example. In *Man the Hunter*, R. Lee and I. DeVore, eds. (Chicago: Aldine), pp. 241–249.

McKern, T. W., and T. D. Stewart, 1957. *Skeletal Age Changes in Young American Males Analyzed from the Standpoint of Identification.* Headquarters Quartermaster Research and Development Command, Technical Report EP–45 (Natick, Mass.).

Peebles, C. S., 1974. *Moundville: The Organization of a Prehistoric Community* (Ph.D. diss., University of California, Santa Barbara).

Peebles, C. S., and S. M. Kus, n.d. Some Archaeological Correlates of Ranked Societies. (Manuscript in preparation, Museum of Anthropology, University of Michigan.)

Rao, C. R., 1952. *Advanced Statistical Methods in Biometric Research* (New York: John Wiley).

Sears, W. H., 1956. Excavations at Kolomoki: Final Report. *University of Georgia Series in Anthropology*, No. 5 (Athens: University of Georgia Press).

Service, E. R., 1962. *Primitive Social Organization: An Evolutionary Perspective* (New York: Random House).

Stewart, T. D., and M. Trotter, eds., 1954. *Basic Readings on the Identification of Human Skeletons: Estimation of Age.* (New York: Wenner-Gren Foundation for Anthropological Research).

Todd, T. W., and C. W. Lyon, 1925. Cranial Suture Closure. *American Journal of Physical Anthropology* 8 : 23–71.

Vallois, H., 1960. Vital Statistics in Prehistoric Populations as Determined from Archaeological Data. In *The Application of Quantitative Methods in Archaeology*, R. F. Heizer and S. F. Cook, eds. (Chicago: Quadrangle Books), pp. 186–204.

Waring, A. J., Jr., and P. Holder, 1945. A Prehistoric Ceremonial Complex in the Southeastern United States. *American Anthropologist* 47 : 1–34.

Weiss, K. M., 1972. On the Systematic Bias in Skeletal Sexing. *American Journal of Physical Anthropology* 37 : 239–250.

———, 1973. *Demographic Models for Anthropology.* Memoirs of the Society for American Archaeology, No. 27, pp. 1–186.

Biocultural Dimensions of Archeological Study: A Regional Perspective

JANE E. BUIKSTRA

THE "new archeology" of the 1960's and the prehistoric cultural ecology of the 1970's have created new roles for the human osteologist in archeological research. This recent emphasis upon the interdependence of human biological, cultural, and physical environmental variables belies a scientific intimacy almost as old as the systematic investigation of prehistoric cultures. Descriptive analyses of skeletal materials have been a traditional part of archeological research, either by design or by necessity, whenever a burial area has been excavated. In most cases, however, the physical anthropologist/osteologist has been viewed primarily as a technician whose ultimate goal is the production of the tables and figures so often relegated to appendices of site reports. However precise and laboriously derived, this type of data infrequently addresses the research goals of the archeologist and is thus neglected in later stages of archeological interpretation.

Recently, attempts to expand the technician's role have become increasingly creative and successful. Pioneer efforts in this direction began long ago, often led by scholars associated with the Smithsonian Institution. Recently, however, renewed interest by archeologists in the social dimensions of mortuary practice and subsistence–settlement systems has served to stimulate participation of bioanthropologists in archeological inquiry. The effort has been further encouraged by the refinement of biological research techniques appropriate for the study of variability in human populations, from the level of microdifferentiation in shape and structure to the study of epidemiology.

In a regional context, the investigation of the human biological system is critical to the investigation and development of local histories and the derivation of deductively testable models of human behavior. While anthropological archeologists develop increasingly complex models of interaction between biological, environmental, and cultural variables, the physical anthropologist frequently can provide unique clues to aspects of social organization, demography, population interaction and relationship, and the efficiency with which temporally sequential paleopopulations have dealt with universal problems of nutrition and disease.

This paper will describe the strategy and contributions of a research program in prehistoric human biology and mortuary site archeology to an ongoing, regionally based study of prehistory. The research reported here includes data derived from studies other than my own, which will be appropriately cited. Any misuse or misinterpretation of these data is unintentional, and I assume full responsibility. Since the goal of this study is to integrate and interpret information presently available in other sources, detailed data sets are not presented here. The reader is urged to consult primary sources for further documentation.

The area in which we are working comprises the lower seventy miles of the Illinois River valley and adjacent uplands. This region is attractive to combined bioarcheological investigation for numerous reasons. First, this has been an area of intensive occupation for several thousand years of prehistory. The potential availability of data from temporally sequential populations is further enhanced by the fact that for at least one thousand of these years mound burial formed the primary—if not exclusive —type of mortuary behavior, thus providing us with discrete and recognizable cemeteries. In addition, the existence of an established program of archeological excavation of habitation sites within the area provides an attractive source of data that may be used as complementary data sets.

This discussion will be directed toward the investigation of populations that inhabited the lower Illinois River region during the period from approximately 150 B.C. to A.D. 1000. The initial part of the occupational sequence is known culturally as the Middle Woodland period, which lasted until approximately A.D. 400. The phenomenon known variously as "Hopewell," "the Hopewell Interaction Sphere," and by other labels, is associated with this period of prehistory. Following Middle Woodland, we have a period traditionally defined by an absence of the elaborate artifacts and monumental structures familiar to students of Hopewell. This more recent period is known as Late Woodland.

The natural environment in the lower Illinois region provided a relatively stable, lush setting for prehistoric groups. Although the effects of paleoclimatic change during the Woodland period require further, systematic evaluation, existing sources doubt that in this area there was a major floral response to climatic change during the period from 150 B.C. to A.D. 1000.[1] It is likely that the range of tubers, roots, and seeds extant today in the Illinois Valley was there in recent prehistory. It is also likely that plant communities, if significantly altered at all by paleoclimatic change, simply shifted their geographic location within the context of linear resource zones parallel to the river, rather than radically altering their composition. Though exploitation patterns differ through prehistory, the composition of faunal samples documented in archeological sites does not show specific differences that would allow one to infer major climatic changes. Thus, for the purposes of this paper, natural resource availability will be assumed to be relatively stable.

Seasonality is a dominant feature of the pattern of local resource availability influencing exploitation efficiency of both plants and animals. Though varying by season from the sap of the sugar maple in spring through herbaceous summer resources to the fruits of the fall, plant resources are notably unavailable throughout the winter, lasting from November to March. The human group is thus especially vulnerable to dietary and disease stress at this time. It is suggested here that the development and control of mechanisms for buffering the effects of this winter "hunger time" comprise a major parameter affecting Woodland adaptations in the region.

Prior to the appearance of significant quantities of maize in archeological context, the pattern of resource exploitation for the Illinois region reflects marked stability. Until the ninth century A.D., when the uplands are reoccupied for the first time since the Archaic, Woodland habitation sites tend to cluster in the main trench of the Illinois River and its largest tributaries (Whatley and Asch 1975). Whatley and Asch (1975) suggest an appropriate model for resource exploitation during the Middle Woodland and early Late Woodland periods. This model involves stable communities whose seasonal cycle of resource procurement ranges over collector territories that become increasingly smaller as site density increases during the early Late Woodland period. Storage pits also increase in both size and frequency at this time. Identifiable change in patterns of resource procurement and utilization reflect increased dependence upon resources within the smaller collector territories of the more recent period.

A new form of regionally based, interdisciplinary research in mortuary site archeology and human osteology has been developed in the course of the present study. With the active participation of both archeologists and physical anthropologists in all phases of research design, members of our "bio-archeological" research group made the initial decision to focus upon the investigation of biocultural change within the Woodland period. Woodland adaptations were selected due to our concern for the great number of unresolved questions centering on the Middle to late Woodland "transition" popularly known as the "decline of Hopewell," which has been variously explained in terms of migrations, climatic change, disease stress, and other factors. Our decision was also tempered by the fact that there already existed a great quantity of data from previously excavated Woodland cemeteries. A high density of relatively undisturbed sites also provided a potential for investigation of additional sites, as appropriate. After the initial decision to focus upon Woodland, phased research was undertaken by each scholar in a manner designed to provide complementary and comparable data for the discussion of the five topics outlined in the center of figure 1.

A major form of field research initiated during the early phases of our study was mortuary site survey. We quickly learned that sites in the region were far more numerous than the published literature would have us believe. We also inferred that after explicitly stating and evaluating our assumptions concerning the completeness of cemetery populations we should be able to investigate paleodemographic patterns previously inaccessible to us.

A further advantage of the data provided by survey involves conservation of archeological resources. In these days of inflation, excavation analysis and curation have become expensive—luxuries we can ill afford if they are not absolutely necessary. Survey becomes, then, a means of conserving our excavation efforts and the archeological record through the precise identification of those sites most likely to provide us the quality and quantity of data needed for our present research. We systematically collect data that indicate soil attributes affecting the preservation of both osseous materials and site structure, as well as elements of site location and external morphology. Subsequent to survey, excavation is viewed as a means of testing hypotheses concerning group size and distribution, as well as a means of procuring burial data and skeletons.

I would also like to emphasize that the ordering of research topics in our design is not arbitrary. Although each subject is of equivalent importance in terms of potential contributions to biocultural research, a programmatic approach to their investigation is crucial. Initial phases should concentrate upon the definition of the prehistoric burial program—the variety and ordering of treatments accorded the dead for the total prehistoric social group. Information concerning the variety of decisions made in the disposal of the dead to some degree reflects status and role differentiation within social groups and is, therefore, intrinsically important. An equally crucial implication, however, centers on the fact that prehistoric groups, through their systematic selection of personal or group attributes in the course of the mortuary ritual, may introduce biases that affect osteological interpretations.

The study of disease and pathology in paleoseries, for example, is an exciting and reasonable goal of osteological research. The most sophis-

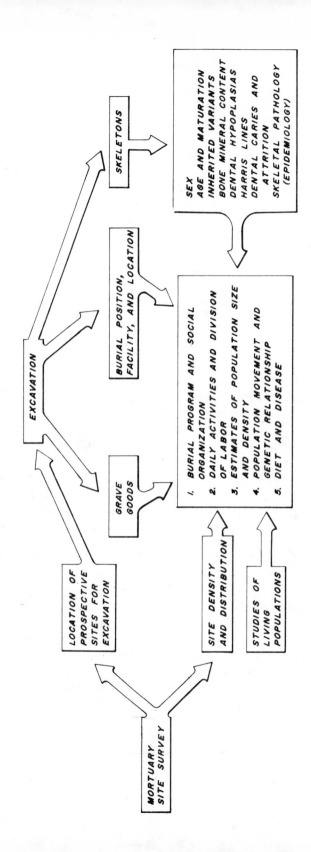

Figure 1. Diagram of interdisciplinary research strategy
in mortuary site archeology and human osteology utilized in this study.

ticated analytical techniques for investigating disease, however, are poorly used for general inferences if the composition of the burial sample is skewed by prehistoric disposal practices that artificially indicate disease states. An illustration of this point may be drawn from the Horizon VI (Archaic) burial sample from the Koster site (Buikstra 1976b). At Koster, individuals excavated from the central midden of Horizon VI comprise the old and abnormally diseased individuals, with the remainder of the population interred elsewhere. For the purposes of investigating the impact of disease states upon Archaic populations of this period, the midden sample is clearly not representative. In order to avoid the risk of sampling biases based upon spatial segmentation of prehistoric practice, the inclusive or representative nature of the cemetery should be investigated prior to any subsequent phase of osteological study. Similarly, biases introduced by differential skeletal preservation should be considered.

Error introduced by diverse burial procedures within a single burial program also affects paleodemographic study. As illustrated above by the Archaic sample, one cannot venture comparisons of archeological populations on the assumption that they are necessarily representative. The inclusive nature of the cemetery must be demonstrated or the missing elements simulated if meaningful comparisons are to be made between local groups.

The next consideration, a critical one prior to extensive epidemiological study, is the study of the inheritable attributes of skeletal morphology. The question of genetic heterogeneity is an important adjunct to the explanation of culturally defined subsets of burials, and the possibility of migration or class endogamy may affect demographic interpretations. In addition, statements concerning disease states and comparative frequencies of nonspecific stress indicators must be prefaced by considerations of biological relationships. In temporally sequential series from a local region, for instance, the modulation of a disease form means something very different when it develops within indigenous groups rather than accompanying marked gene flow. It is well known also that the response to both disease and generalized stress can vary from population to population. Therefore, the strength of epidemiological statements must be tempered with a consideration of biological relationships within and between the archeological series.

I will now turn from the research design to the data on Middle to Late Woodland populations, groups exemplifying both change and stability. The Middle to Late Woodland "transition" has been broadly characterized in the literature as a period of marked cultural change. Basing inferences largely upon elements of artifact style and burial disposition, researchers have depicted the Late Woodland period as a "dark ages," or a period of cultural "decline" prior to the Mississippian Renaissance (for example, see Griffin 1964). It is becoming increasingly apparent, however, that most aspects of Woodland lifestyle show a great deal of stability, even in the lower Illinois River region, an area well known for the association of diagnostic Hopewell items with Middle Woodland. Utilizing the research strategy outlined above, I would like to examine an array of biocultural attributes for Middle and Late Woodland, emphasizing the development of predictive behavioral models and the integration of biological and archeological data.

MIDDLE WOODLAND

We have initially developed a biocultural model for Middle Woodland against which we may contrast Late Woodland. Since these data have been detailed elsewhere (Buikstra 1972; Tainter 1975), only the following summary statement of propositions and supporting information will be presented here.

1. *Mounds comprised the major identifiable disposal facility during the Middle Woodland period.* (This proposition is a critical definition of the inclusive and representative nature of all burial and skeletal data.) In assessing the validity of this statement, we have (*a*) identified the Middle Woodland burial program, emphasizing the definition of intermediate stages located outside the mounds; (*b*) systematically tested for nonmounded cemeteries near Middle Woodland mounds; (*c*) compared mortality profiles and life tables derived from cemetery samples with model tables generated from contemporary data; and (*d*) evaluated estimates of Middle Woodland population density and distribution against ethnographic accounts (Buikstra 1972).

2. *Middle Woodland communities represent stable occupation of sites evenly spaced along watercourses.* This proposition has been examined through the investigation of (*a*) site distribution (Struever and Houart 1972), and (*b*) inherited morphological attributes (Buikstra 1972).

3. *Within the local Middle Woodland community, a system of social ranking can be identified.* Variables that limit access to the most exclusive and expensive forms of burial treatment have been defined. In that all individuals of a specific age and sex do *not* have equal access to all tracks of the burial program, various systems of ranking have been suggested (Buikstra 1972; Tainter 1975).

4. *It may be inferred that individuals of paramount rank controlled resource redistribution, including a variety of economically important*

items. This proposition is tentatively confirmed by the differential distribution of burial accoutrements and attributes of skeletal morphology that may reflect access to scarce resources (Buikstra 1972; Tainter 1975).

In sum, Middle Woodland communities existed as relatively stable local groups spaced along the main trench of the Illinois River and its tributaries. Individuals of paramount rank, as defined by access to Hopewell items, probably controlled redistribution of these items within the community, as well as the movement of these items through supralocal interaction. It is also probable that items of local manufacture and food resources followed similar control and redistribution patterns.

LATE WOODLAND

Late Woodland societies can be compared and contrasted to the above Middle Woodland groups, utilizing the biocultural model. Before extending the discussion to the question of change within the Woodland milieu, however, we must once again evaluate the relative completeness of our skeletal samples. For the earliest Late Woodland sites, there is an indication that burial procedures other than mound interment formed a regular part of the burial program. For instance at the Pete Klunk site, males are clearly underrepresented (Tainter 1975). The presence of nonmounded crematories (Buikstra and Goldstein 1973) and other burial features peripheral to Late Woodland mounds also suggests that sampling biases may have affected the composition of cemetery samples and that our data should be regarded as minimum "best estimates" for many of the parameters discussed below.

1. *Social Organization.* The conspicuous absence of exotic items from mortuary context has caused archeologists to emphasize the apparent differences between Middle and Late Woodland burial procedures. Although forms of burial treatment do vary—cremation, for instance, is added to the Woodland burial repertoire during the Late Woodland period—the complexity of site organization for the earlier portion of the Late Woodland period is of the same order of magnitude as that for Middle Woodland (Tainter 1975[2]).

This similarity in complexity of burial programs suggests a stability and/or continuity of social complexity for Middle Woodland and early Late Woodland local groups. Given other data concerning the diminished importance of supralocal resource redistribution during early Late Woodland, we would anticipate that control of local collector territories would have been assuming increased importance in systems of ranking. However, the contrast between levels of complexity in Middle Woodland—

early Late Woodland and that defined by Tainter (1975) for the latter part of the Late Woodland period (post A.D. 800)—is notable and convincing. This coincides generally with the appearance of significant quantities of maize at habitation sites and perhaps is associated with increased importance of land control as a means of defining rank. Interpretations such as these of Late Woodland burial programs are in preliminary stages at this time and conclusions are necessarily tentative. However, the current data do suggest that the most striking change in social organization occurred within the Late Woodland period rather than at its inception.

2. *Genetic Relationship and Breeding Isolates.* The patterning of inherited attributes of skeletal morphology indicates stability and continuity for temporally sequential Middle and Late Woodland populations. Nonmetric traits of the cranial and postcranial skeleton have been compared, utilizing eight Woodland series. The C. A. B. Smith distance statistic (D_c), modified to minimize effects of missing data, was used in a series of two-way comparisons.[3] A single Mississippian series (from the Schild site) was included for comparative purposes.

If we utilize an average-link clustering technique to associate those sites showing greatest morphological similarity, i.e., minimal "biological distance" as measured by the Smith statistic, we may then isolate patterns of association as they vary in time and space. A superimposition of site linkages upon a geographic mapping of site location would clearly indicate that a major factor affecting morphological dissimilarity in these series is geographic distance. Sites isolated by time but not by space tend to share patterns of nonmetric trait frequency. The converse is not true. This osteological pattern would be consistent with a hypothesis of stable local gene pools. Certainly, it seems that population movement would have little explanatory power in reference to the archeologically defined cultural differences between Middle and Late Woodland.

It should be noted, however, that these sites do not, of course, exist on a Euclidian plane. There are, in the research area, diverse environmental factors that may, alternatively, facilitate or restrict various forms of interaction, including gene flow. The Mississippi and Illinois river valleys and the intervening uplands, which expand in breadth as one moves north, are two obvious natural discontinuities.

One means of evaluating the effect of these geographic factors on gene flow is to compare the correlation of our epigenetic distance measure with both straight geographic distance and distance as measured by river-miles (table 1). The results of this comparison clearly indicate that the correlation of epigenetic distance with river-miles is greater than that with straight linear miles during Middle Woodland times. This is not the

Table 1.
Correlation of Epigenetic Distance Statistic (D_e)
With Geographic Distance

	Pearson R Statistic	
	Straight Line Geographic Distance with D_e	River Distance with D_e
Middle Woodland	0.5818	0.8785
Early Late Woodland ca. A.D. 600–700	0.9619	0.9951
Later Late Woodland A.D. 800–1000	0.9912	0.9912

case for both early and late Late Woodland series. Here straight geographic distance and river miles explain comparable amounts of variability in epigenetic distance.

Orientation to the river as a factor facilitating gene flow changes from
the Middle to Late Woodland periods. The pattern described here would
be consistent with a Middle Woodland model of populations spaced along
the rivers and oriented to it as a means of mediating interaction. Subsequently (during the Late Woodland period), simple geographic distance
explains an amount of variability comparable to that for river miles.
Effective interactive space apparently becomes circular rather than linear, perhaps with increased exploitation of upland regions. From these
skeletal data alone we may not speculate concerning size of the effective
breeding isolate. However, on the basis of other information presented
in this paper, one might expect these data to form part of a set describing marked population increase and relative localization of gene pools
during the Late Woodland period. The nonmetric data certainly would
not be inconsistent with such a model.

We will examine here two aspects of demography: regional population density and group composition. Both, to some extent, reflect elements of adaptive success, although neither can be adequately evaluated without recourse to other bioarcheological attributes.

3. *Regional Population Density.* We can generate relative estimates
of population density for the lower Illinois region on the basis of data
defining mortuary site density, combined with data providing osteological
information. Estimates of site density have been based upon survey data
from DeRousseau (1974). Our previous information concerning the inclusive nature of burial samples derived from mounds indicated that
mound burial formed the dominant disposal type for both Middle and

Late Woodland structures; we may—by generating an estimate of site density, temporal association, and burials per mound—estimate regional patterns of population density for the period in question. The assumption that most if not all mounds are Woodland is justifiable, although a few Archaic structures have been identified. In accord with our definition of the early Late Woodland burial program, estimates for that period should be considered as a minimum.

Given the assumptions detailed above, we have developed a demographic model utilizing information from both excavated and unexcavated sites. Estimates of temporal association, numbers of burials, and mean age at death have been used to develop a preliminary estimate of prehistoric population density and distribution for Middle and Late Woodland groups.

The details of this analysis are reported elsewhere by DeRousseau (1974). We may summarize her findings briefly by noting that the population estimate supports an hypothesis of steady population increase through time. Given the fact that our estimate for early Late Woodland is a minimum one, there is evident here no striking population increase associated with any segment of the Late Woodland period, although indications of increased site and burial density are convincing. Further, if we assume that the variable distribution of burial population reflects intraregional distributions of local groups, we find that there is a marked increase in the number of individuals living (being buried) on the east side of the river throughout the Late Woodland period. It is tempting to associate this pattern with a shift in subsistence-maintenance activities, resulting in a steady increase in population density for areas which have maximal access to arable land, either in the floodplain or in the upland.

4. *Group Composition.* Death rates for juveniles and adults have been examined here separately, according to the techniques developed by Cook (1976). For juveniles, our expectation is that increased death rates due to biologically stressful conditions will be disproportionately distributed among age classes. This follows a demographer's device for measuring malnutrition levels in contemporary populations for which census data is of poor quality. We would predict, following this model, that relatively malnourished groups should show greater mortality experience during ages one to four years, than for other juvenile ages. Initially, within and between population comparisons for four juvenile ages (0–1 years, 1–4 years, 5–9 years, 9–14 years) were examined for a significant difference in the Middle versus Late Woodland comparisons that is not evident in within-period tests. An increased number of Late Woodland individuals in the weanling age sample strongly suggests that the prehistoric lifeway during Late Woodland times was more biologi-

cally stressful than that for precedent populations in the same area. These conclusions must, however, be tempered by the observation that the degree to which the Late Woodland curve departs from the models may indicate factors affecting the composition of the sample other than mortality experience. Tests by Cook have not isolated a source of either natural or cultural bias for these populations.

Middle and Late Woodland adult mortality profiles also show directional trends. Survivorship curves indicate that probability of survival for Middle Woodland young adults is markedly greater than that for later populations. Comparison with the model tables generated by Weiss (1973) indicates that life expectancy at age fifteen was five years less for Late Woodland individuals than for a Middle Woodland cohort of the same age.

When combined, the juvenile and adult data from Cook's work (1976) are mutually reinforcing and congruent with a model of increased biologically stressful conditions during the Late Woodland period.

5. *Drift-Maize Agriculture.* A shift in subsistence from Middle to Late Woodland is not unexpected, given other data directly derived from skeletal analysis. Our only information to date, pertaining to our most direct measures of dietary composition (the variables of strontium content, caries, and attrition rates), have been collected from only Middle and late Late Woodland sites (Brown 1973; Cook and Buikstra 1973; Cook 1976). Antoinette Brown (1973) described late Late Woodland Indians as being more herbivorous than Middle Woodland individuals, on the basis of increased amounts of stable strontium found in bones from the more recent sites. Cook and Buikstra (1973) have indicated that enamel defects of the deciduous dentition in post-weanling juveniles have significantly more caries in later groups, with age of caries onset earliest among adults, as well (Cook 1976). Conversely, attrition rates are greater for the Middle Woodland groups. The pattern here strongly suggests increased carbohydrate content for the later Late Woodland diet. The increased attrition rate for Middle Woodland may reflect either dietary differences or contrastive food preparation techniques.

6. *Infectious Disease.* The prehistoric populations of the lower Illinois valley provide numerous examples of the striking, proliferative reaction areas of the skull and long bones that have long excited speculation concerning pre-Columbian trepanematosis.[4] Epidemiologic patterning for these lesions recently has been studied by Cook (1976), who concludes that, although the pathology does not precisely mirror the expected bony expression of any contemporary infection, the closest is with a general treponemal model. However, there is no indication that

the disease was a venereal pathology. It is also important to note that there is a slight indication that the disease is modulating from a chronic, progressive, and not highly virulent form during Middle Woodland times to an acute, more lethal expression by the latter part of the Late Woodland period (Cook 1973). At this time, it is not certain whether this transformation should be associated with the early or the late Late Woodland period. Larger samples of early Late Woodland materials should clarify the tempo of these epidemiologic changes.

7. *Generalized Stress Indicators.* We may divide our nonspecific osteological markers of biological stress into groups: (1) those that reflect acute episodic upset and recovery, and (2) those that are associated with chronic stress. Our data are limited at this time, to a single Middle Woodland series and one late Late Woodland sample. Differences in patterning for the two forms of pathology, however, are identifiable and thus provide an added dimension to both demographic and infectious disease data.

(*a*) *Acute stress.* Attributes reflecting acute stress which have been analyzed for these groups include Harris lines in both adult (Rawlins n.d.) and juvenile samples (Cook 1976). In addition, enamel hypoplasia in deciduous dentition has been examined by Cook and Buikstra (1973). Frequencies for these indicators have been analyzed in association with mortality schedules, in order that interpretations would not be biased by bone remodeling or selection against individuals who suffer from acute stress episodes.

Both forms of osseous lesions that reflect acute, episodic stress show increased frequencies in Middle Woodland samples. There is, also, some suggestion that selection may operate against Late Woodland weanling juveniles whose history includes the stresses reflected in the hypoplastic defects. Thus, the frequency of defects for the Late Woodland mortality sample may be inflated above that for the total cohort. This makes the presence of the higher frequencies of hypoplastic defects in the earlier groups particularly striking. It should be noted, however, that the pattern of weanling selection does not exist in the Harris line data, although larger samples and improved radiographic techniques may suggest an alternative model. In any case, the emergent pattern from the present data suggests that episodic stress and recovery was more frequent among Middle Woodland populations than for groups of the later Late Woodland period.

(*b*) *Chronic stress.* Maturation rate, as measured by the linear regression of femur length against dental age, indicates that the late Late Woodland individuals were attaining adult stature less rapidly than ear-

lier populations. This indication of increased chronic stress is supported
by trend toward decreased cortical thickness in the femora of Late
Woodland juveniles (Cook 1976). Thus, the data reflecting episodic
stresses are not redundant with those representing chronic conditions.
Mortality experience, representing the cumulative disease and malnutrition history of an individual, appears to co-vary with chronic rather than
acute stress.

The proper interpretation of these data, in association with those reflecting subsistence strategy, specific disease, and demography, must be
approached with caution. At first examination, one might want to emphasize the contrast of acute and chronic stress indicators, emphasizing
that the benefits of more predictable resources (maize during Late Woodland) included relative freedom from episodic stress and the ability to
support relatively large populations. The costs of this dependability include decreased longevity, epidemic disease, and chronic forms of stress
(probably including chronic malnutrition). It must be remembered however, that osteological measures of acute stress actually reflect recovery
from the stressful episode and that contemporary populations undergoing chronic stress do not show high frequencies of Harris lines. The
inadequate nutritional pattern thus masks the effects of disease episode,
psychosocial stresses, and others, by decreasing the probability of a recovery stage. In this way, the quality of nutrition has increased the load
upon the biological system to the point that additional, episodic stress is
not recorded skeletally unless the effect is terminal. Thus, for the populations reported here, one would want to emphasize the biological costs,
including indications of acute disease stress and malnutrition, rather than
the benefits of the Late Woodland lifeway(s).

8. *Intergroup Violence.* Perino (1973a, 1973b, 1973c) has reported
numerous instances of Late Woodland skeletons found with projectile
points lodged in bones or associated with the body cavity. He infers that
intergroup strife and competition was keen throughout this period. There
is a virtual absence of identifiable cases of deaths that may have resulted
from similar circumstances for the Middle Woodland period. However,
it should be remembered that small projectile points that are likely to
be retained in soft or hard tissue are not a part of the Middle Woodland
artifact assemblage. Thus, our Middle Woodland estimate of active intergroup violence is biased by factors that would not affect Late Woodland data. However, given the well-documented presence of structured
interaction between social groups during the Middle Woodland period,
the inverse relationship of archeologically recoverable evidence of intergroup violence to exchange networks is not unexpected.

SUMMARY AND CONCLUSIONS

We may now return to our original research problem: the investigation of biocultural change during Middle and Late Woodland times. To
say that "yes, there *was* change" clearly understates a rather complex,
ongoing interrelationship of biological and cultural variables. Those upon
which we have concentrated here may be summarized by the following
listing:

1. *Social Organization*: increased complexity identifiable during latter part of Late Woodland period.
   (*a*) *Supralocal Resource Redistribution*: characteristic of Mid-
        dle Woodland.
   (*b*) *Settlement Pattern*: change occurs with occupation of
        uplands, ca. ninth century A.D.
2. *Breeding Isolates*: spacing was apparently more closely tied to
   geographical, rather than social, distance throughout Late Woodland period.
3. *Population Density*: steadily increased throughout both periods.
4. *Group Composition*: mortality rates.
5. *Maize Agriculture*: apparent at, or around, ninth century A.D.
6. *Infectious Disease*: possible increased incidence of violent form
   during Late Woodland period.
7. *Generalized Stress Indicators*:
   (*a*) *Acute Stress Markers*: only late Late Woodland and Mid-
        dle Woodland population studied. Decrease through time.
   (*b*) *Chronic Stress Markers, Stable Strontium Content, Acute,
        Infectious Disease*: only data available at this time con-
        trasts Middle with late Late Woodland. Increase in all
        three through time.
8. *Intergroup Violence*: positive evidence begins during early Late
   Woodland period.

Figure 2 schematically presents the pattern of association for these
variables, as they reflect biocultural change during the Middle and Late
Woodland periods. Identifiable directional changes are indicated by +
and −, with open markers displaying patterns altered in association
with the Middle Late Woodland interface. Encircled markers illustrate
modulations, either documented or inferred, within the Late Woodland
period. The left side of the diagram illustrates the relatively early reor-
ganization of biosocial spacing and resource redistribution pattern, which
was followed by pronounced transformations in subsistence strategy,
social complexity, and quality of life.

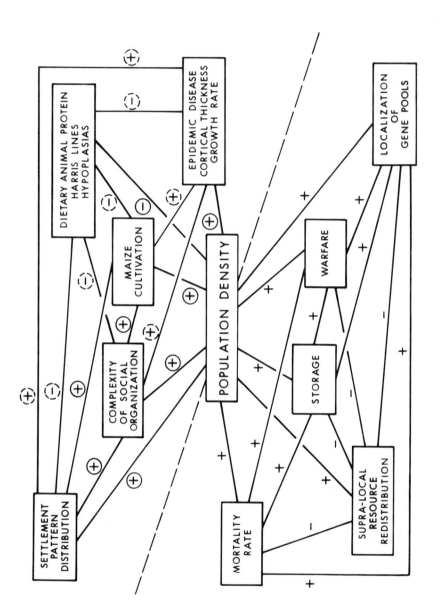

Figure 2. Schematic Diagram Indicating Relationship of Biocultural Variables Utilized in this Study.

Clearly, the purpose of this paper has not been to identify any single factor responsible for the "decline of Hopewell." With a concern for prehistoric ecological relationships, the focus has been systemic rather than particularistic. The emphasis has been upon the identification of relationships between variables which reflect prehistoric social organization, subsistence strategy, demography, and biological relationship. Data from mortuary sites and skeletal series have been utilized, displayed against a regional setting. The nature of this research design has directed the efforts of cooperating scholars toward involvement in multiple phases of archeological inquiry, including the initiation of extensive survey programs through which we hope to conserve our excavation energy, while refining our ability to define mortuary behavior on a regional scale. The models presented here for Middle and Late Woodland should be considered tentative and *must* certainly be refined through further survey, excavation, and laboratory analysis. However, with these preliminary results, we hope to have successfully affirmed the importance of a bioarcheological perspective in the study of prehistory.

NOTES

1. See Zawacki and Hausfater (1960) for a discussion of prehistoric plant communities and their composition.
2. Tainter notes a diminution of rank by one level from Middle to Late Woodland and infers a decrease in social complexity. The significance of this statement is questionable, however, in light of the fact that, as mentioned before, there is strong evidence for spatially distinct burial areas during early Late Woodland. These have not been incorporated into Tainter's model. It is clearly possible that one or more social ranks may have been interred in a situation that would have excluded them from Tainter's analysis.
3. See Buikstra (1972) for an attribute listing and explicit statement of methodology. It should be noted here that lower frequency traits have been eliminated and that the smallest population comprises 28 individuals.
4. The four commonly recognized modern trepanematoses are venereal syphilis, endemic syphilis, pinta, and yaws.

REFERENCES

Brown, A. B., 1973. *Bone Strontium Content as a Dietary Indicator in Human Skeletal Populations* (Ph.D. diss., University of Michigan).
Buikstra, J. E., 1972. *Hopewell in the Lower Illinois River Valley: A Regional Approach to the Study of Biological Variability and Mortuary Activity* (Ph.D. diss., University of Chicago).
———, 1976. Koster Site: Prehistoric Human Ecology. In *The Koster Site:*

A Progress Report. Evanston: Northwestern University Archaeological Program, Special Report No. 1.

Buikstra, J. E., and L. Goldstein, 1973. Perrins Ledge Crematory. Illinois State Museum Reports of Investigations No. 28 (Springfield, Ill.).

Cook, D. C., 1973. Woodland Indians in Illinois: Disease in Biocultural Perspective. (Paper presented at the annual meeting of the American Anthropological Society, New Orleans, La.)

————, 1976. *Pathologic States and Disease Process in Illinois Woodland Populations: An Epidemiologic Approach* (Ph.D. diss., University of Chicago).

Cook, D. C., and J. E. Buikstra, 1973. Circular Caries: A New Tool in Nutritional Assessment in the Past. (Paper presented before the 42nd annual meeting of the American Association of Physical Anthropologists, Dallas, Texas.)

DeRousseau, C. J., 1973. Mortuary Site Survey and Paleodemography in the Lower Illinois River Valley. (Paper presented before the annual meeting of the American Anthropological Association, New Orleans, La.)

Griffin, J. B., 1964. The Northeast Woodland Area. In *Prehistoric Man in the New World*, J. Jennings and E. Norbeck, eds. (Chicago: University of Chicago Press).

Perino, G., 1973a. The Late Woodland Component at the Pete Klunk Site, Calhoun County, Illinois. In *Late Woodland Site Archaeology in Illinois I*. Urbana: Illinois Archaeological Survey Bulletin No. 9, pp. 58–89.

————, 1973b. The Late Woodland Component at the Schild Sites, Greene County, Illinois. In *Late Woodland Site Archaeology in Illinois I*. Urbana: Illinois Archaeological Survey Bulletin, No. 9, pp. 90–140.

————, 1973c. The Koster Mounds, Greene County, Illinois. In *Late Woodland Site Archaeology in Illinois I*. Urbana: Illinois Archaeological Survey Bulletin No. 9, pp. 141–206.

Rawlins, R., n.d. An Analysis of Harris Line Formation in Two Temporally Distinct Woodland Populations. (Manuscript on File at Northwestern University Osteology Laboratory.)

Struever, S., and G. Houart, 1972. An Analysis of the Hopewell Interaction Sphere. In *Social Exchange and Interaction*. Ann Arbor: Anthropological Paper No. 46, Museum of Anthropology, University of Michigan, pp. 47–79.

Tainter, J. A., 1975. *The Archaeological Study of Social Change: Woodland Systems in West-Central Illinois* (Ph.D. diss., Northwestern University).

Weiss, K. M., 1973. *Demographic Models for Anthropology*. Society for American Archaeology, Memoir 27, pp. 1–186.

Whatley, B., and N. Asch, 1975. Woodland Subsistence: Implications for Demographic and Nutritional Studies. (Paper presented before the annual meeting of the American Association of Physical Anthropologists, Denver, Colo.)

Zawacki, A. A., and G. Hausfater, 1969. *Early Vegetation of the Lower Illinois Valley*. Springfield: Illinois State Museum Reports of Investigations No. 17.

Applications of Trace Element Research to Problems in Archeology

ROBERT I. GILBERT, JR.

RESEARCH concerning the role of trace elements in biological organisms began in the early part of the twentieth century, but only within the last thirty years have the profound effects of trace elements upon the growth, development, morbidity, and mortality of *Homo sapiens* been recognized (Underwood 1971). Deficiencies or surpluses of trace elements in human diets have been implicated in dwarfism, mental retardation, hypertension, atherosclerosis, goiter, and many other afflictions (Schroeder 1973). It is becoming increasingly evident that certain trace elements, heretofore either disregarded or unknown from a nutritional perspective, are essential for the production and maintenance of healthy animals and plants.

The promising potential of trace element analyses of skeletal materials is of interest to the paleonutritionist/archeologist. From observations of differing amounts of some trace elements in bones, it may be possible to deduce the presence of dietary stress and its possible consequences of reduced disease resistance, retarded growth, and retarded development. In addition, variations of skeletal content of these elements may permit insight into status differences; the separation of sexes, ages, and social classes; the introduction and adoption of classes of (or of specific) cultigens; and the overall effects of these upon the population, should a site offer sufficient time depth.

These attractive prospects are based upon the ability of bone to absorb, at varying levels, trace elements available to the organism through its food and water intake. While bone does not accept all elements, nor tolerate some elements beyond its genetically programmed homeostatic levels, there remains a degree of leeway that permits some elements to be incorporated at levels possibly reflective of their intake in the diet.

TRACE ELEMENTS

Approximately 98 percent of the "standard" or "reference" human body (70 kg.) is composed of oxygen, carbon, hydrogen, nitrogen, calcium, and phosphorus in respective descending order of total percentage contribution. Of importance, but lesser concentration, are potassium, sulfur, chlorine, sodium, magnesium, and iron. Trace elements are defined as those occurring in amounts of less than 0.01 percent of the human body mass (Schroeder 1973 : 13). To qualify as an essential trace element, Cotzias (1967 : 5) suggests that the following criteria be met:

1. it is present in all healthy tissues of all living things;
2. its concentration from one animal (same species) to the next is fairly consistent;
3. its withdrawal from the body induces reproducibly the same structural and physiological abnormalities regardless of the species;
4. its addition either prevents or reverses these abnormalities;
5. the abnormalities induced by deficiency are always accompanied by pertinent specific biochemical changes;
6. these biochemical changes can be prevented or cured when the deficiency is prevented or cured.

Trace elements have been divided into three groups (Underwood 1971 : 2): those that are considered dietary essentials; those that are possibly essential; and those that are, insofar as known, nonessential. The ten essential trace elements are: iron (Fe), iodine (I), copper (Cu), zinc (Zn), manganese (Mn), cobalt (Co), molybdenum (Mo), selenium (Se), chromium (Cr), and tin (Sn). Nickel (Ni), fluorine (F), bromine (Br), arsenic (As), vanadium (V), cadmium (Cd), barium (Ba), and strontium (Sr) are usually classed as possibly essential. Magnesium (Mg) is not included in Underwood's scheme of essential trace elements due to its higher concentration in the body, but it most certainly is a metabolically essential element.

Although trace elements are necessary for the proper growth, development, and reproduction of all animals and plants, the species of the animal or plant determines the relative proportions and amounts of these elements. It is precisely this feature of differential use and absorption that permits some generalizations about the trace elements and their applicability to the investigations suggested previously.

Many trace elements are differentially stored and utilized by flora and fauna, but for the purposes of the paleonutritionist/archeologist it is necessary that these trace elements also be ones that are present in bone, given the more probable occurrence of hard tissue remains on a site. This necessitates the selection from the "master list" of elements those that are known to "fix" or accumulate in bone tissue. Some of these, e.g., lead, are cumulative and will increase within the bone for as long as the element constitutes some portion of the animal's intake by means of ingestion, respiration, or direct external contact. Others appear to "fix" in bone, but only up to certain levels, at which point the majority (or surplus beyond the homeostatic needs of the organism) of the intake is excreted in the urine, hair, perspiration, nails, and feces. Although the exact capacity of bone for certain elements has not been determined, it appears that—with the exception of those that "fix" so firmly *and* are cumulative—a range of presence may be found in the bone, suggesting a consumption of the trace element that may vary in amounts up to maximum capacity. The proposition of both some "capacity" and some difference in concentration is drawn from Cotzias' second criterion that the element in question is fairly consistent from one animal to another.

Insufficient research on trace elements, particularly in regard to bone metabolism and absorption, precludes the presentation of a definitive list of the elements that might assist the archeologist, but there is adequate information to suggest that the following may be profitable. Most plants possess higher concentrations of Mg, Mn, Sr, Ni, and Co per unit of mass than do animals. The majority of animals, however, display greater amounts of Zn, Cu, Mo, and Se.

A comparison of the concentrations for some of the trace elements according to category of food stuffs is provided in table 1 (Schroeder, personal communication). It should be recognized in the construction of such a table that the use of the mean for these categories does not imply that the trace element is distributed evenly throughout the plant or animal, for some plant structures and animal organs will concentrate the element in greater quantities than others.

As can be observed from the table above, Zn, Cu, Mg, Mn, Mo, and Sr offer greater possibilities of differentiating among the categories of food sources than do Se, V, and Co. The researcher should not be dissuaded from investigation of those of lesser concentration, for, indeed, they may offer greater insights into his particular nutritional problem. However, it is suggested that Cu, Zn, Mg, Mn, and Sr, are perhaps the most amenable to diet discrimination with the least possibilities of error of analyses (not to mention complexities of techniques).

Table 1.

Mean Elemental Concentrations in Parts per Million (ppm)
for Grains, Vegetables, Meats, and Nuts

Element	Grains and Cereals	Vegetables*	Meats**	Nuts
Manganese	7.00	2.50	0.20	17.00
Copper	2.00	1.20	3.90	14.80
Zinc	17.70	6.00	30.60	34.00
Magnesium	805.00	307.00	267.00	1970.00
Strontium	3.00	1.90	2.00	60.00
Vanadium	1.10	1.60	—	0.71
Cobalt	0.43	0.14	0.22	0.47
Molybdenum	1.79	0.51	4.82	—
Selenium	0.15	—	0.92	—

   * Category of vegetables includes values for legumes, tubers, and leafy material.
   ** Category of meats excludes fish and shellfish.
   — Indicates the absence of sufficient data.

PALEONUTRITIONAL APPLICATIONS

In making an assessment of a contemporary population's nutritional status, it is possible for the nutritional anthropologist to collect relatively precise data on the specific types and amounts of foodstuffs consumed, the rate of morbidity (possibly mortality), and the height and weight of individuals. The ability to estimate the caloric intake and expenditure, together with these other measures, obviously offers a sound basis for nutritional status judgment.

Such documentation of the nutritional status of an archeological population is usually far more difficult. The archeologist is more frequently limited to analyses of faunal and floral remains found on, or around, the site of the excavation. Under certain geographic and climatic assumptions, it is possible to posit a dietary reconstruction based upon the contemporary fauna and flora of the region. Ecological reconstruction of archeological diets entails collection, counting, and identification of the various remains with a view toward establishing their relative importance in the nutritional intake of the populations. The most serious restrictions incurred by such methods are the presence and identifiability of the floral and faunal remains. Under certain conditions of preservation, most commonly in arid climates, estimations of the diet may be made from the fecal material of the inhabitants. Regrettably, at many archeological sites, there may not be sufficient botanical or zoological evidence from which dietary estimates can be generated. Thus, instead of augmenting the proposed reconstruction of the population's diet with inferences from social organization and technological implements, the archeologist may be reduced to the most tentative of suggestions.

Even in the absence of sufficient animal and plant remains, the archeologist has other methods for nutritional assessment. If there is a reasonable abundance of skeletal material available, it is possible to deduce the presence of nutritional stress from differential mortality, morbidity (estimated from skeletal pathologies), carious lesions, and statural changes over time. These methods, effective as they may be, do not necessarily permit the paleonutritionist insights into the specific nature of the dietary stress unless sufficient faunal and floral matter accompanies the skeletal material.

Trace elements in bone are increasingly becoming subjects of investigation; however, most of the attention has centered upon their effects and processes within soft tissues as related to disease and nutrition. Fortunately, some contemporary research has been directed to the establishment of varying levels of trace elements in bone (Becker et al. 1968; Spadaro et al. 1970). Schroeder, Tipton, and colleagues have published extensive reports containing information about trace elements in humans, including bone.

Three recent studies have explored the potentialities of trace element concentrations in bone as a tool for paleonutritional/archeological research. Employing strontium, Parker and Toots (1970) demonstrated that within a particular site, levels of Sr in bone, tooth enamel, and tooth dentin are consistent in the remains of a single species. Brown (1973) attempted the discrimination between high- and low-status individuals from several archeological sites, utilizing the ratio of Sr to Ca. Performing analyses of Zn, Cu, Mg, Mn, and Sr, Gilbert (1975) demonstrated the probability of a dietary shift from hunting and gathering to maize cultivation at an Amerindian site. These studies suggest that the use of trace element analyses may serve the archeologists/paleonutritionists well in their attempts to evaluate the predominant components of prehistoric diets.

The use of trace elements to assist in dietary specification is fraught with difficulties. Although a number of trace elements can be associated predominantly with either plant or animal origin, there are few elements in which the separation is sufficiently great to permit the *immediate* association of a specific animal or plant with the concentration found in the skeletal material analyzed. Nuts and berries are particularly susceptible to confusion with animal sources (for some elements), inasmuch as germinating parts usually contain much higher concentrations of trace elements (see table 1).

To enhance the security of the conclusions drawn from such analyses, it is imperative that the researcher be aware of interactions and possible complexing of the trace elements being considered (O'Dell 1967; Dowdy et al.1969; Underwood 1971). For example, Zn and Cu are antagonistic, so it might be expected that should Zn intake decline, Cu concentrations might well increase. Oberleas et al. (1969) and O'Dell (1972) have also explored the interactions between Zn and phytate (a common component of cereals and grains), concluding that the presence of phytate markedly decreases the availability of Zn to the organism.[1] Such conditions, while confusing, do not necessarily present impediments to the researcher, for they may provide the exact clue to his or her selection of elements for analysis as well as confirmation of tentative archeological suppositions.

Given these caveats, is it possible to offer some elucidations of prehistoric diets? For this question to be approached, it is necessary to establish some analytical specifications. These include: (*a*) the archeologist must have some realistic (if vague) conception of the probable composition of the diet; (*b*) the acidity of the soil that forms the matrix of the excavated material must be minimal (pH > 5) to assure minimal ionic replacement or activity; (*c*) ideally, the animal and plant sources potentially available to the population should be identified correctly as to species and probable numbers; and (*d*) the degree of permanent residence of the population at the place of excavation should, insofar as possible, be known.

Quite naturally, it would appear that if the archeologist were cognizant of each of the above he or she could well generate a dietary approximation that would be reasonably accurate. However, in many cases this is not possible. Should, for example, the site offer some animal skeletal material along with some apparently cultivated grains, is he or she in a position to determine whether the animal remains are supplements to an essentially grain diet, the other way around, or whether the two are equally balanced? If the artifacts are too few, as in the example presented, or if they are absent, such determination may be impossible.

Certainly, the analyses of trace elements cannot supplant archeological observation and data, but rather the two in tandem may reveal insights of dietary consumption that either alone could not afford. It is fully recognized that the analysis of trace elements is time-consuming, and perhaps expensive, depending upon the circumstances and choice of methods.[2] Further, if the archeological data are extremely clear, such analyses may be unnecessary. This paper is directed to those instances in which resolution of the dietary components cannot be obtained by more traditional means, as well as to those occasions when additional supportive evidence is desired.

If the conditions mentioned above (particularly soil pH > 5) can be met, then the utility of trace element analysis becomes obvious. Should the archeologist be confronted with a skeletal population whose diet (from the evidence) could be predominantly vegetarian, animal protein, or equally balanced, trace element analyses of the skeletal material might resolve the question, but only in terms of those broad categories. However, under certain assumptions, trace element analyses might also be capable of further discriminations. For example, should the archeologist have reason to believe that he or she is dealing with a stratified society that may have dictated access to certain foodstuffs to its members, again in the broad category of animal versus vegetable, trace element analyses of the individuals, when compiled with burial position, goods, etc., may well be able to confirm the suspected social divisions.

The primary concern of this paper is not addressed to the nutritional essentiality or the effects of deficiency or abundance of trace elements as demonstrated by skeletally observable pathologies. However, it seems appropriate to indicate briefly an outline of such nutritional and metabolic effects that are known. The identification of trace element deficiencies in man has been quite limited, although experimental evidence from plants and animals suggests that all organisms display some consequences according to the severity of deprivation. In the natural state deficiencies of only five trace elements (Zn, Cu, Mg, Fe, and I) have been reported for man (Underwood 1971). Three of these (Zn, Cu, and Mg) will be discussed with regard to the effects of variation of metabolic availability in the following section.

The elements proposed as potential discriminators of diet (Zn, Cu, Mg, Mn, Sr, Mo, V, Co, Se, and Ni) are not all found in analytically "comfortable" quantities. This is due either to their availability in the diet, which is relatively uncommon, or to some form of metabolic discrimination against their absorption into bone. From this list, only four of the elements (Zn, Cu, Mg, and Sr) will be considered. This certainly does not imply that the remainder are unimportant, for they may be used to good advantage depending upon the particular problem confronting the researcher. In most cases, however, they occur in such small quantities in bone that the analyst is presented with both technical difficulties and a potentially expensive undertaking.

Of the trace elements suggested for dietary analyses, and for potential verification by archeological means, zinc ranks foremost in its implications. While the various biochemical roles of zinc have not been completely elucidated, it is well documented that zinc is a necessary mineral for proper mineralization of bone (Haumont and McLean 1966), for endocrine functions (Miller et al. 1968), wound healing (Pories and Strain 1966), disease resistance (Weinberg 1972), and growth (Prasad 1966). Healthy human bone contains approximately 181 ppm of Zn (Gugenheim and Gaster 1973). Generally adequate amounts of zinc for human diets can be derived from both animal and vegetable sources, but some populations depend heavily upon cereals or grains for the bulk of their caloric intake. As previously mentioned, the action of phytate interferes with the proper absorption of what zinc is available from the cereal/grain, as well as with any zinc ingested from other sources at the same time. This creates a reduction, if not deficiency, in the total diet. This reduction/deficiency possibly may be displayed in an archeological population by decrease in stature, increased rates of pathologies, and mortality over a period of time. The work of Pories and Strain and that of Weinberg is of particular interest in this context. Pories and Strain (1966) have demonstrated that a reduction in the amount of available zinc delays the closure of wounds and subepidermal tissue healing. This lengthens the period of time available for pathogens to penetrate the body's defenses. Weinberg (1972) suggests that a reduction of trace elements metabolically accessible to the organisms results in increased susceptibility to pathogens and parasites which, once established, begin to compete with the body for these elements. Such findings are evidently of utility to the paleonutritionist/archeologist in suggesting that he or she examine the dietary potentials for sources and reductions in zinc.

Copper is one of the most crucial trace elements for the production and survival of healthy animals and plants. Its prime function appears to be in the reduction of molecular oxygen to water by means of copper enzymes acting as electron transfer oxidases (Schubert 1964). For humans, sufficient copper is usually available, with healthy bone tissue averaging 19.63 ppm (Cartwright and Wintrobe 1964). However, Cordano et al. (1964) have shown that copper deficiencies can and do occur in humans. These deficiencies were associated with hypoproteinemia. Although the meaning is yet uncertain, Cu serum levels are elevated during severe chronic disease experiences, as well as in the presence of neoplasms, hepatic disorders, and anemias. It is not suspected that a severe Cu deficiency would exist in a population, but it is possible that a decrease in the availability and amount of Cu intake may contribute to increased stress. This is based on the knowledge that serum Cu is elevated during disease and if the mobilization of Cu is a resistance reaction, then a diminished availability of Cu from the diet may reduce the capacity to resist or promptly recover from a prolonged disease experience.

In human bone, strontium concentrations range around 114 ppm (Sowden and Stitch 1957). The rate of mineral turnover in bone, for most elements, is greater during the first years of life. Consequently, metabolic discrimination against Sr increases with age. While the precise role of Sr in metabolic activities has not been determined, several researchers have demonstrated that Sr can function as an aid to calcification and initiate apatite formation as well as possibly enhancing the resistance of dentin and enamel to carious lesions (a function also attributed to Mo and Se). The availability of Sr in various foods suggests that a deficiency in human diets is most unlikely, and, with the exception of severely distorted experimental diets, Sr absorption does not appear to be subject to antagonism by other trace elements. Sr has been shown to accumulate with age (Schroeder et al. 1972). Thus, varying levels of Sr intake may be reflected by Sr concentrations in bone, depending upon the amount of vegetable foodstuffs ingested (Rivera 1967).

The normal concentration of magnesium in healthy human bone is approximately 1,100 ppm (Schroeder et al. 1969). Concentrations decline with age for most of the body tissues except for the aorta. This decline takes place predominantly during the first ten years of life and the amount of Mg remains relatively consistent thereafter (Tipton et al. 1969). Although not common, magnesium deficiencies do occur in humans, usually arising from malfunctions of the parathyroid and thyroid glands and alcoholically induced excretion. There is also some indication that Mg deficiency may accompany protein-calorie malnutrition, but this is more likely to result from the absence of calories than the lack of protein (Drenick et al. 1969). The symptoms of magnesium deficiency frequently are revealed in various dysfunctions and debilitations of the nervous system. The regulation of the magnesium/calcium ratio appears to be partially responsible for the correct development of healthy bone tissue, for too little Mg encourages the deposition of Mg in skeletal muscle and other soft tissues. As populations continue to discover and employ methods of food refining, it is possible that the quantity of dietary Mg will decline. Prehistoric populations presumably did not live under Mg deficient stress, inasmuch as their technology for refining foodstuffs would have been minimal, and there is rarely evidence that they lacked an adequate caloric intake. The utility of Mg stems primarily from its abundant occurrence in vegetable matter, and thus it may be employed as a dietary component indicator.

METHODS

In selecting bones for trace element analyses, it is suggested that those having the thickest cortical dimensions be employed. This measure provides for two contingencies: (*a*) depending upon the pH of the soil and the length of the time the material has remained in the ground, cortical bone is less susceptible to leaching and permeation than cancellous bone, which permits more ready access to groundwater flow-through; and (*b*) thick cortical bone also offers the advantage of "averaging" over the entire sample thickness, which increases the probability of obtaining readings that more accurately reflect the dietary consumption over longer periods of time. The exclusion of *both* endosteal and periosteal surfaces, which can be scraped away using nonmetallic instruments (e.g., glass slides), reduces the risk of the analyses containing the areas of greater metabolic activity in bone turnover that might skew the results.

The researcher has at least four investigative techniques available to him or her for trace element analyses of bone and other materials.[3] Each of the following techniques possesses certain advantages and disadvantages, depending upon both the information sought and the degree of precision desired.

1. *Atomic Absorption Spectroscopy*. Of all methods available, this one offers the fewest technical complications as well as the greatest range of accuracy. The equipment is inexpensive, compared to the others, and most universities have one or more units on campus. No more than two grams of the material to be analyzed are needed, and sample preparation is quite simple. With regard to bone, the sample may either be "wet" ashed (i.e., using an acid directly to dissolve the sample) or "dry" ashed by placing the sample in a muffle oven for 24 hours or longer at 400°C until it is sufficiently reduced to go into solution with the acid easily. The decision of which ashing technique to employ is best determined empirically. Obviously, the "wet" ashing method is less time-consuming. Prior to this it is suggested that the bone be pulverized to assist in its reduction. Hollow cathode lamps are available for most of the natural elements and analyses may proceed quickly. A disadvantage of the method is that only one element may be analyzed at a time. For the investigator seeking several elements (and depending upon the number of samples), atomic absorption can consume quite a bit of time. Additionally the method demands the destruction of the sample. On the positive side, atomic absorption is quite sensitive even at 10 ppm and can determine smaller concentrations for some elements.

One of the drawbacks for atomic absorption involves the detection of trace elements that are not expected to be more than 2–10 ppm in concentration within the bone. The flow rate through the aspirator necessitates the use of a greater amount of the sample than for elements of higher concentrations. This circumstance applies to the use of the flame absorption method. The graphite furnace method is available and consumes far less of the sample than the flame technique, but it is also more subject to the complexing or obscuring of some elements than the flame method. If the researcher decides in favor of using the graphite furnace, he or she must ascertain that the readings obtained are both consistent and reflective of the true concentration. At present, the better method is the use of the flame technique, provided that there is sufficient sample available to permit the longer running time through the aspirator.

2. *Emission Spectroscopy.* While it is possible to obtain quantitative figures from this method, at best they are estimates made against a known standard. Should the researcher desire only a display of the elements contained with the samples, emission spectroscopy is a better method than atomic absorption. Given that the researcher is not concerned with absolute amounts, emission spectroscopy offers an excellent technique for determining the elements present, as well as their approximate concentrations. This method is also very satisfactory for ratio analysis. Thus, the researcher can request ratios of Zn to Cu, Ca to Sr, or any particular combination desired, provided that a ratio will be sufficient to the solution of the problem under investigation. The ratio method potentially complicates the problem, by requiring the knowledge of the interaction (specifically of the elements involved in the ratio, as well as potential interactions with the elements not so concerned). While the technique is less sensitive than atomic absorption, it does provide the researcher with the advantage of being able to analyze for any number of elements at the same time. Sample preparation is simple, entailing the pulverization of the bone, but it also commits one to the destruction of the sample. Emission spectroscopy requires slightly more of the sample if one allows for repeated observations than does atomic absorption. The equipment for this procedure is also available in most analytical chemistry laboratories.

3. *Electron Microprobe.* The major disadvantage to this technique is the rarity of the equipment. Its sensitivity is above approximately 20 ppm, depending upon the element being tested, but it has the advantage of not destroying the sample. A disadvantage is that sample preparation is perhaps more tedious than other methods discussed. While the electron microprobe technique produces no noticeable effects upon the sample, in most cases some destruction of the bone will occur in the process of obtaining the sample in the first place. The electron micro-

probe is perhaps most useful to the investigator in determining if the bone has been subjected to discernible leaching or differential replacement of the requisite trace elements. This can be determined by taking a cross-section of the bone (i.e., a transverse cut that encompasses both the periosteal and endosteal surfaces) and scanning across the section from one surface to the other. If the obtained readings indicate extensive variability of the elemental concentrations, then some form of elemental disturbance is indicated.

4. *Neutron Activation.* This relatively new technique possesses all of the virtues of the previous methods and few of the disadvantages. Essentially the analysis consists of exposing the sample to a neutron flux, thereby creating a high energy state in the material. As the newly formed isotopes begin to decay, the emitted particles are counted (half-life decay) and amounts of the elements calculated. Neutron activation offers the most precise of trace element determinations without the destruction of the sample, other than in its original acquisition. Very few universities, however, possess the equipment, and the costs of analyses are quite high. This method should perhaps be utilized only when extremely critical precision is demanded.

DISCUSSION

Knowledge of the interactions and effects of trace elements upon disease resistance and growth and development may well lead to improved estimates of a population's nutritional and health status. Such information could assist in the mapping of the prehistoric spread of various cultigens and diseases. It might also be possible to plot the adoption/ deletion of certain sociocultural traits. For example, status differentiation may be indicated by trace element differences based on disproportionate access to specific food sources. Additional consideration should be given to the antagonism between and among some of the trace elements, as the presence of antagonisms can aid the researcher in detecting the addition or deletion of certain foodstuffs in the diet.

There are certain aspects of trace element analyses that must be satisfied before the dietary applications can be employed with surety. If the problem is simply to distinguish between predominantly animal or vegetable diets, it can conceivably be solved with little question. However, if one seeks to determine the relative proportions of the dietary constituents, then the amount of each trace element considered and its available sources must be clearly detailed. It should be remembered that plants, like animals, will accumulate trace elements that are found in their environment. Thus, the trace element composition of various plants is, within limits, dependent upon the soil chemistry in which they are growing. One must first consider the time depth under investigation and then estimate or empirically determine whether the genetic stock of the contemporary flora and fauna in the region is identical to that of the material associated with the level of excavation. Further testing of the soil, plants, and animals must be made to discover the degree of variation of trace element absorption by the organisms of both periods. With the assembly of such data, it is then possible to construct educated estimates of the relative proportions of the various foodstuffs consumed by a population from the amount of the trace elements found in the bones. The preceding is predicated on controls for leaching or permeation from the surrounding matrix.

This strongly suggests that it is imperative that data be collected on the trace element composition of plants, berries, nuts, barks, etc., of contemporary plant material by geographic area as quickly as possible. The introduction of industrial pollutants, as well as the wide distribution of chemical fertilizers, is rapidly reducing the possibilities of even the tentative assumptions that the plants of today are of similar or identical genetic stock and possess the same levels of trace elements as did those of prehistoric periods. Without this information, it will be very difficult to reconstruct the specific composition of prehistoric diets.

Animals whose diet consists of only one or two identified dietary items can be analyzed for declines in one or more specific trace elements associated with their dietary sources. This in itself may provide some indirect evidence of the trace element content of various food items available to a population. Analyses of different species of animals found on a site (if their dietary habits are sufficiently well documented) may offer an indirect method of obtaining information about the quantity of certain trace elements constituting their dietary basis, and that may well have been exploited by man.

A further potential of trace element analysis, while not of direct dietary concern, is its application to environmental and ecological issues. While no hard and firm data exist on all trace elements and their benefits or hazards to humans, analyses of archeological material for selected elements (e.g., Hg, Pb, Te, and Cd) may provide much needed baseline information regarding the "natural" or preindustrial condition of humans. Obviously, such an undertaking must be restricted to the most careful controls of the environment and the habitat of the source materials employed for comparison. The resulting information could offer to colleagues in contemporary human biology new realms for ecological and environmental studies.

Many of the subtleties of trace elements are yet to be known, but at the present time sufficient information and techniques are available to the paleonutritional researcher to prompt serious examination of this potential tool. If all of the precautions and methodological considerations are observed, it is doubtful that the researcher can be misled solely on the basis of trace element analyses. Hence the technique can serve only to clarify, if not resolve, many of the questions pertaining to the diet under consideration.

NOTES

1. Phytic acid or inositol hexaphosphoric acid is present in some legumes and nuts, but mostly in the husks of cereals. Phytic acid combines with Ca, Fe, Zn, and Mg derived from other dietary sources, rendering these elements to some extent insoluble and nonavailable.

2. Editor's note: At most commercial laboratories, costs for atomic absorption analysis of calcium, magnesium, manganese, and zinc run between $7.50 and $10.00 per ½- to 1-gram sample and $2.50 to $3.00 for each additional element. Neutron activation, the most expensive of the techniques described by Gilbert, can run as high as $100.00 per sample for the first element and increments of $6.00 to $8.00 for each additional element. However, many departments of chemistry and physics at major universities already utilize the above techniques and, depending on policy, may provide trace element analysis free or at reduced rates to institutionally affiliated researchers.

3. For more complete descriptions and discussions of the analytical methods presented, the reader is directed to Cescas et al. (1968), Reynolds and Aldous (1970), Robinson (1966), Weissberger and Rossiter (1972), and Willard et al. (1975).

REFERENCES

Becker, R. O., J. A. Spadaro, and E. W. Berg, 1968. The Trace Elements of Human Bone. *The Journal of Bone and Joint Surgery* 50A:326–334.

Brown, A. F. B., 1973. Bone Strontium Content as a Dietary Indicator in Human Skeletal Populations (Ph.D. diss., University of Michigan).

Cartwright, G. E., and M. M. Wintrobe, 1964. Copper Deficiency in Infancy. *Pediatrics* 34:324–326.

Cescas, M. P., E. H. Tyner, and L. J. Grey, 1968. The Electron Microprobe Z-Ray Analyzer and Its Use in Soil Investigations. In *Advances in Agronomy*, No. 25, A. G. Norman, ed. (New York: Academic Press), pp. 153–198.

Cotzias, G. C., 1967. Importance of Trace Substances in Environmental Health as Exemplified by Manganese. *Proceedings of the University of*

Missouri's First Annual Conference on Trace Substances in Environmental Health (Columbia: University of Missouri).

Dowdy, R. P., G. A. Kunz, and H. E. Sauberlich, 1969. Effect of a Copper-Molybdenum Compound upon Copper Metabolism in the Rat. *Journal of Nutrition* 99:491–496.

Drenick, E. J., I. F. Hunt, and M. E. Sivendseid, 1969. Magnesium Depletion During Prolonged Fasting of Obese Males. *Journal of Clinical Endocrinology* 29:341–348.

Gilbert, R. I., 1975. Trace Element Analyses of Three Skeletal Amerindian Populations at Dickson Mounds (Ph.D. diss., University of Massachusetts).

Guggenheim, K., and D. Gaster, 1973. The Role of Manganese, Copper and Zinc in the Physiology of Bones and Teeth. In *Biological Mineralization*, I. Zipkin, ed. (New York: Wiley), pp. 443–462.

Haumont, Z., and F. C. McLean, 1966. Zinc and the Physiology of Bone. In *Zinc Metabolism*, A. S. Prasad, ed. (Springfield: Charles C Thomas), pp. 169–186.

Miller, E. R., R. W. Luecke, D. E. Ullrey, B. V. Baltzer, B. L. Bradley, and J. A. Hoefer, 1968. Biochemical Skeletal and Allometric Changes Due to Zinc Deficiency in the Baby Pig. *Journal of Nutrition* 95:278–286.

Oberleas, D., M. E. Muhrer, and B. L. O'Dell, 1966. The Availability of Zinc from Foodstuffs. In *Zinc Metabolism*, Z. S. Prasad, ed. (Springfield: Charles C Thomas), pp. 225–238.

O'Dell, B. L., 1967. Dietary Interactions of Copper and Zinc. *Proceedings of the University of Missouri's First Annual Conference on Trace Substances in Environmental Health* (Columbia: University of Missouri).

———, 1972. Dietary Factors that Affect Biological Availability of Trace Elements. In *Geochemical Environment in Relation to Health and Disease*, H. C. Hopps and H. L. Cannon, eds. Annals of New York Academy of Science, No. 199, pp. 70–81.

Parker, R. B., and H. Toots, 1970. Minor Elements in Fossil Bone. *Geological Society of America Bulletin* 81:925–932.

Pories, W. J., and W. H. Strain, 1966. Zinc and Wound Healing. In *Zinc Metabolism*, A. S. Prasad, ed. (Springfield: Charles C Thomas) pp. 378–394.

Prasad, A. S., 1966. *Zinc Metabolism* (Springfield: Charles C Thomas).

Reynolds, R. J., and K. Aldous, 1970. *Atomic Absorption Spectroscopy, A Practical Guide* (New York: Barnes and Noble).

Rivera, J., 1967. Predicting Strontium-90 Concentrations in Human Bone. In *Strontium Metabolism*, J. M. A. Lenihan, J. F. Loutit, and J. H. Martin, eds. (New York: Academic Press), pp. 47–55.

Robinson, J. W., 1966. *Atomic Absorption Spectroscopy* (New York: Marcel Dekker).

Schroeder, H. A., 1973. *The Trace Elements and Man* (Old Greenwich, Conn.: Devin-Adair).

Schroeder, H. A., A. P. Nason, and I. H. Tipton, 1969. Essential Metals in Man: Magnesium. *Journal of Chronic Diseases* 21:815–841.

Schroeder, H. A., I. H. Tipton, and A. P. Nason, 1972. Trace Elements in Man: Strontium and Barium. *Journal of Chronic Diseases* 25:491–517.

Schubert, J., 1964. *Copper and Peroxides in Radiobiology and Medicine* (Springfield: Charles C Thomas).

Sowden, E. M., and S. R. Stitch, 1957. Trace Elements in Human Tissue. Estimation of the Concentrations of Stable Strontium and Barium in Human Bone. *Biochemistry Journal* 67:104–109.

Spadaro, J. A., R. O. Becker, and C. H. Bachman, 1970. The Distribution of Trace Element Ions in Bone and Tendon. *Calcified Tissue Research* 6:49–54.

Tipton, I. H., P. L. Stewart, and J. Dickson, 1969. Patterns of Elemental Excretion in Long-term Balance Studies. *Health Physics* 16:455–462.

Underwood, E. J., 1971. *Trace Elements in Human and Animal Nutrition* (New York: Academic Press).

Weinberg, E. D., 1972. Infectious Diseases Influenced by Trace Element Environment. In *Geochemical Environment in Relation to Health and Disease*, H. C. Hopps and H. L. Cannon, eds. Annals of the New York Academy of Science, No. 199, pp. 274–284.

Weissberger, A., and B. W. Rossiter, eds., 1972. *Physical Methods of Chemistry*, Vol. I, Part IIID, *X-Ray, Nuclear, Molecular Beam, and Radioactivity Methods* (New York: Wiley-Interscience).

Willard, H. H., L. L. Merritt, Jr., and J. A. Dean, 1975. *Instrumental Methods of Analyses* (Princeton: Van Nostrand).

Teeth as Tools for Prehistoric Studies

ANTHONY J. PERZIGIAN

PREHISTORIC populations, like modern ones, adjusted to environmental changes in two basic ways. The first was genetic adaptation, and the second, nongenetic adaptation, for example behavioral, physiologic, and developmental. Both modes of adaptation can be profitably studied through examination of the teeth of prehistoric groups. Research on heritability has shown, for example, that the size and morphology of teeth are strongly determined by genetic factors; thereby, microevolutionary changes can be studied. Teeth, furthermore, are developmentally plastic structures and respond sensitively to environmental conditions during growth. In essence, they represent milestones of growth and development and permit one to view stress-related adjustments during ontogeny.

This paper focuses, then, on dental studies as an approach critical to a full understanding of earlier human populations—their biology, their behavior, and their affinities to other groups. First, the value and potential of dental studies are accented by reviewing some recent work on prehistoric groups; second, a new methodological approach for assessing prehistoric environmental stress is offered.

SOME APPLICATIONS OF DENTAL ANTHROPOLOGY

There are three different types of studies reported here. These are (a) histologic and chemical, (b) morphologic, and (c) metric.

Histologic and Chemical Studies. Analyses of the microstructure of histologic features of the dentition have proved potentially valuable for the study of prehistoric populations. Since human teeth do not grow once erupted, they permanently record systemic irregularities during growth. If environmentally induced stresses are severe, they result in zones of hypomineralization in the enamel and dentin. Such hypoplasias may stem from metabolic disturbances that affect embryonic calcification. Known sources of disturbances are nutritional deficiencies and infectious disorders. Comparative histologic studies should yield valuable data on health, diet, and environmental conditions of prehistoric groups.

Studies along these lines include those of Molnar and Ward (1975), who compared microsections of molars from several prehistoric Indian populations from California to Michigan and reported histologic differences between agricultural and nonagricultural groups. Variations between the groups appeared to be related to geographical and cultural factors. Rose (1973) employed the frequency of histologic defects to estimate the disease experiences of three Illinois groups representing the transition from hunting and gathering to agriculture. He argued that this transition resulted in higher sociopsychological stress levels, lower protein availability, and greater exposure to pathogens. His data tentatively suggest that histologic defects increased through time. Together, these works support earlier observations (Sognnaes 1956) that microstructural defects of the dentition are common throughout the human skeletal record. An association between culture and dental defects, while not yet unambiguously established, does seem likely.

Plans are now being formulated by the Brookhaven National Laboratory to test prehistoric human teeth for the presence of trace elements. With the method of charged particle x-ray excitation, rapid and reliable qualitative analyses can be performed that provide informative data on (*a*) the health status of early populations and (*b*) the effects of technicoindustrial change on the biological uptake of trace elements. Are there associations between various metals industries and tooth chemistry? Can we detect the polluting effects of mining activities and campfires on prehistoric people? Trace element analysis may provide the answer.[1]

Finally, scanning electron microscopy offers opportunities for studying the diet and food preparation technology of past populations. Shkurkin and associates (1975) have developed a technique for making photomicrographs of molar occlusal surfaces. They report differences in ultrastructural wear between Paleo-Indians from California and contemporary American whites. The abrasive diets of the Indians apparently produced deep, multidirectional scratches and obliterated the normal "punch-board" morphology of the enamel. Clearly, more comparative studies of this kind are needed to clarify further the association between biology and culture.

Morphologic Studies. Unraveling the natural history of prehistoric Indians is possible if the following requirements are met: (*a*) valid measurements of microevolution and (*b*) accurate assessment of population affinities. Satisfaction of these requirements can be approached through morphologic dental traits. Authors have stressed that dental crown features have a strong genetic component (Turner 1967); recent refinements suggest that morphologic traits, for instance, incisor shoveling, cusp number, Carabelli's cusp, are quasi-continuous variables that stem from multiple genes and environmental factors (Lombardi 1975; Bailit 1975).

To test and confirm the value of tooth morphology in distinguishing population differences, Sofaer and associates (1972) compare biological distances based on dental traits with geographic distances and estimates of genetic difference calculated from blood group frequencies. Tooth morphology was in moderately good correspondence with the geographical distances separating and the gene frequencies distinguishing the Zuni, Pima, and Papago populations. Turner (1967) earlier reported good agreement between serological and dental data that indicated European admixture in an Eskimo population. Most recently, Brewer-Carias and associates (1976) observed for the Yanomamo and Makiritare good agreement between a matrix of pairwise "dental distances" and corresponding matrices based on eleven genetic systems and on geographic location. Hence, it seems that tooth morphology is a good indicator of genetic affinities among populations.

Other investigators have recognized the utility of morphologic dental traits as genetic markers. Moorrees (1951) attributed differences between two Aleut populations to white admixture. Tarahumara Indians could be distinguished from neighboring Mestizos by morphologic traits (Snyder et al. 1969). Smith (1973) compared closely related patrilineages of Habbanites from southern Israel who lived in identical environments. In the latter study, various morphologic traits accurately discriminated the groups and indicated considerable genetic drift. Perhaps hypotheses regarding prehistoric social structure can be tested by comparing the tooth morphology of individuals classified by position or location of interment in a mound.

Hypotheses explaining the demise of a population can also be tested. Austin (1970) found little temporal variation for eleven dental traits from a series of Mayan populations; he concluded, therefore, that no other groups had intruded and disrupted the local genetic continuity. Morphologic trait analysis was also used by Turner (1971) to demonstrate three separate waves of aboriginal migrants into the New World. Indeed, as genetic markers, morphologic dental traits are valuable reservoirs of information about the biological relationships among prehistoric groups.

Some investigators have stressed the adaptive value of dental traits. For example, Greene (1972) and Mayhall (1975) claimed that, with the increased consumption of cariogenic foods, natural selection would favor teeth with less complex fissure patterns and fewer cusps. Hrdlička (1920) and Dahlberg (1963) suggested that shovel-shaped incisors are structurally superior where mechanical stresses are severe.

Due to typically severe occlusal attrition, morphologic data are quite difficult to collect from the dental crowns of prehistoric groups. Molnar (1972) has exhaustively reviewed the literature on dental attrition and indicated the need for more systematic study. His work (1971) on New World groups has shown that the degree and type of wear differ between agricultural and nonagricultural groups; this interpopulation variation reflects diet, food preparation techniques, tool usage, and sexual division of labor. That variation is associated with material culture and diet has also been confirmed by Lavelle (1970) and Wolpoff (1971). Whether through mastication, chewing hides, or cracking open mollusks, attrition reflects the daily and intimate contact of prehistoric groups with their environments. In short, valuable information on the nature of early human interaction with the environment can be secured through comparative studies of dental attrition.

Metric Studies. With odontometric data, much too can be learned of adaptation and microevolution in prehistoric populations. For example, Brace (1967; n.d.) has argued that profound changes in human cultural adaptation have altered selective pressures on the dentition. With an agricultural subsistence economy and the attendant changes in diet and food-processing technology, the survival advantage of large teeth was apparently eliminated. He has supported this argument with metric data from the New World and the Far East, and LeBlanc and Black (1974) provide corroborative evidence from the eastern Mediterranean area. Yet, where attrition remains heavy among food-producing people, selection apparently has operated to stabilize or increase tooth size. The author has shown that, among the protohistoric Arikara of South Dakota, individuals from sixteen through twenty-nine years of age tended to have larger teeth than individuals from six through fifteen (Perzigian 1975). Selection probably best accounts for the larger teeth in older individuals of a skeletal population.

Scott (1974) has also demonstrated an evolutionary trend for larger teeth in a series of pre-Columbian Peruvian populations where occlusal attrition increased through time; moreover, in a study of fifty-seven anthropoid species, Hylander (1975) attributed the enlarged incisors of some species to an adaptive response necessary to increase wear potential. The survival value of an efficient (wear-resistant) masticatory apparatus is strongly suggested by Mumma and Quinton (1970), who reported gastric distress in a clinical population lacking posterior tooth occlusion, and by Kapur and Okubo (1970), who reported weight loss and poor health in laboratory rats whose posterior teeth had been surgically extracted. Future studies relating tooth size, diet, and material culture will surely improve our understanding of the adaptive patterns and health status in prehistoric populations.

Apart from genetic changes produced by selection, environmental factors can also account for rapid, secular changes in human tooth size. For a contemporary Ohio population, an improved nutritional status seemingly resulted in the larger teeth of offspring when compared to their parents (Garn et al. 1968); Goose (1971) reported essentially the same dietary effect on British families. Prehistoric culture change resulting in dietary change could thus be traced in dental metric studies. For example, the biological consequences of rapid acculturation—for example, adopting agriculture—can be studied in local skeletal series where good stratigraphic control is maintained. Prehistoric social stratification resulting in some castes enjoying more nutritionally dependable diets than others may account for some synchronic variation in tooth size within groups. Since teeth are both ontogenetically and phylogenetically plastic structures, they are ideal for studies of both short- and long-term adaptive responses in prehistoric populations.

Finally, metric data are potentially valuable for paleodemographic studies. For example, construction of sex-specific life tables is often difficult when skeletal remains are too fragmentary or too commingled to permit sex assessments. Using multivariate discriminant functions derived from tooth measurements, Ditch and Rose (1972) could, in the Dickson Mounds site, accurately sex individuals who had incomplete dentitions. They wisely cautioned, though, that the accuracy of their method rests upon the comparability of the sample from which the functions were derived to the sample for which the functions are employed. Estimates of inbreeding along with population size and structure may also be approached through dental metrics. Metric variation of the highly inbred Tristanites was shown by Bailit (1966) to be significantly greater than that of more outbred groups. However, conflicting data have been published elsewhere (Rosenzweig and Smith 1971).

FLUCTUATING DENTAL ASYMMETRY

The concern of this paper now shifts to a new approach for studying the developmental biology of prehistoric populations. In the preceding discussion, the size and microscopic structure of human teeth were shown to be affected during growth by extrinsic, environmental factors, for instance, nutrition and disease. Experiments on rats have shown that tooth size is directly influenced by dietary deficiencies of protein (Di-Orio et al. 1973) and vitamin A (Paynter and Grainger 1956). For the house mouse, Tenczar and Bader (1966) estimate that somewhat more than 20 percent of the variation in width of second mandibular molars is due to nongenetic, prenatal factors. Hence, metric traits of the dentition clearly reflect the milieu in which an organism is developing and growing.

When environmental conditions are adverse or stressful during growth, the natural bilateral symmetry of the dentition may be disturbed; as a result, inequalities in the size of antimeres are produced. Siegel and Doyle (1975) have shown experimentally that audiogenic stress on pregnant rats increases the magnitude of dental asymmetry in their progeny. Bailit et al. (1970) and DiBennardo (1973) offer data from living human populations that link tooth size asymmetry and environmental stress: dental asymmetry is greatest among those whose health, nutritional, and general socioeconomic status is lowest. Very little is known about specific causes of asymmetry in humans, and only little attention has been devoted to prehistoric groups (Suarez 1974; Sciulli and Carlisle 1975). The author has further examined the association between dental asymmetry and environmental stress by comparing skeletal populations ranging from prehistoric to modern times. It appears that dental asymmetry is an important new tool for estimating the health and nutritional status of prehistoric populations.

Odontometric data were taken from the Late Archaic population at the well-known Indian Knoll site (Oh 2) in west central Kentucky, the late Mississippian population at the Campbell site (Pm 5) in southeastern Missouri, the protohistoric Arikara population at the Larson site (Ww 2) in northern South Dakota, and the Hamann-Todd cadaver population housed at the Cleveland Museum of Natural History. Dental asymmetry is thus investigated in populations that differ on the basis of nutrition, health status, growth, and, ostensibly, exposure to environmental stress. The term *stress* is used in a manner suggested by Cowgill (1975). Stress is ". . . the extent to which an individual experiences deprivation or injury because, by his own biological and cultural criteria, his access to important resources is too limited or too unreliable" (Cowgill 1975: 127).

For the Indian Knoll population, several lines of evidence suggest that population pressure and environmental stresses were severe. Archeological data point to the predominance of shellfish in the Late Archaic diet (Winters 1969). Yet compared to deer, turkey, and drumfish, which were exploited less intensively, shellfish are poor sources of calories, protein, and fats (Parmalee and Klippel 1974). Of note, Late Archaic people also heavily exploited a few nut-bearing species, especially hickory. Yet its maximum reliability is seasonally confined to periods of collection during the late summer and early fall. Pollen studies indicate natural fluctuations in the availability of hickory and walnut and an overall decline in abundance during the closing centuries of the Late Archaic (K. Vickery, personal communication). In a narrow-spectrum economy like that of Indian Knoll (Winters 1974), depletion of an essential food resource could be contributory to its "collapse." The far from optimal diet at Indian Knoll is also indicated by skeletal and dental evidence. Cassidy (1972) recorded the number of Harris lines of growth arrest in the tibiae of 110 individuals; the range was from 2 to 25 with an average of 11.3 per individual. The regular occurrence of the lines clearly indicates seasonal episodes of food scarcity. Furthermore, 89 percent of her sample displayed enamel hypoplasia. A poor nutritional status is also suggested by the high rate of neonatal mortality—20 percent of the population died during the first year of life (Johnston and Snow 1961).

Finally, Cohen (1975) has offered a number of criteria that may be indicative of prehistoric population pressure, for example, an imbalance between a growing population and its resources. That the Late Archaic economy at Indian Knoll was centered around the intensive collection of shellfish and nuts apparently satisfies two of Cohen's criteria whereby a hunting and gathering population (*a*) shifts from the consumption of organisms at high trophic levels to a greater concentration on eating plant foods and (*b*) increases its concentration on water-based resources relative to land-based resources, especially where the resources are shellfish. This argument for demographic pressure at Indian Knoll cannot be conclusively proved until more is known of the preceding Middle Archaic nutritional profile. The skeletal data, though, serve as conclusive, unequivocal testimony of severe growth-limiting factors at work on the Indian Knoll people.

The nutritional ecology of the Campbell and Larson populations was evidently superior to that of Indian Knoll. The former groups developed thriving, dependable economies in part based on agriculture. The cultivation of maize, beans, and squash was supplemented by hunting that contributed significantly to both groups' prosperity (Wedel 1961; Lehmer and Jones 1968; Hurt 1969; Smith 1974). By many criteria, the Campbell and Larson populations enjoyed generally more favorable circumstances than Indian Knoll. These include the rise of populous, stable settlements, development of complex politicosocial organization, and participation in networks of waterborne commerce. Of note, the adult stature of Indian Knoll was smaller than that of either the Campbell or Larson groups. Cook (1971) has shown, in fact, that the rates of long bone growth are lower for Indian Knoll than for later farming groups. It would seem, then, that exposure to growth-limiting factors was greater at Indian Knoll in comparison to Campbell and Larson, where hunting supported an agricultural economy. Finally, as indicated by rich inventories of material goods, a wealth of nonutilitarian items, and prosperous villages, the Campbell and Larson groups represent, respectively, the "highwater marks" of native culture in the Mississippi and Missouri river valleys. These two groups are sufficiently similar (P. J. Watson, personal communication) to be combined into one sample for the purpose of comparison to a preagricultural population.

To the nearest 0.1 mm., mesiodistal and buccolingual measurements were taken on the total permanent dentition of four groups—Indian Knoll ($N=156$), Campbell ($N=73$), Larson ($N=165$), and Hamann-Todd ($N=88$). To express the magnitude of metric asymmetry, several workers (Van Valen 1962; Bader 1965; Bailit et al. 1970; Sciulli and Carlisle 1975) have used correlation coefficients (r) between pairs of antimeric teeth. Correlations were computed on all sixteen pairs of the adult permanent dentition. The proportion of intraindividual variation due to asymmetry is equal to $1-r$ (Bailit et al. 1970). This difference estimates the amount of variation due to nongenetic, environmental factors that have deflected an organism off its course toward bilateral symmetry. When failures to develop symmetrically are random or nondirectional (favoring neither side), the condition is termed fluctuating asymmetry (Van Valen 1962). Such fluctuating inequalities in the size of antimeres probably arise during early development and presumably stem from adverse environmental conditions that have interfered with normal morphogenesis (Biggerstaff 1975). Hence, the degree of asymmetry expresses the level of stress to which a population is exposed during growth.

Elsewhere, the author (n.d.) has shown that directional asymmetry is absent in the various groups. Fluctuating asymmetry, therefore, primarily accounts for the size differences between antimeres. In addition, the sexes were not shown to differ significantly in asymmetry; hence, they were pooled for population comparisons.

In table 1, the mean correlation coefficients of the eight pairs of antimeres from each jaw are presented. Population differences in the proportion of intraindividual variation due to fluctuating asymmetry may be obtained by subtracting the mean total r's in the table. Compared to the Campbell/Larson sample, Indian Knoll is more asymmetrical by 3.5 percent in the mesiodistal dimension and 4.3 percent in the buccolingual dimension. Indian Knoll, by very similar values, is more asymmetrical than the Hamann group.

Table 1.

Mean ($\overline{\mathrm{X}}$) Correlation Coefficients between Antimeres

Teeth	*Indian Knoll* $\overline{\mathrm{X}}r$	*Campbell/Larson* $\overline{\mathrm{X}}r$	*Hamann* $\overline{\mathrm{X}}r$
Mesiodistal			
Maxilla	0.819	0.834	0.820
Mandible	0.825	0.880	0.885
Total	0.822	0.857	0.853
Buccolingual			
Maxilla	0.866	0.890	0.882
Mandible	0.810	0.872	0.871
Total	0.838	0.881	0.877

With Wilcoxon's signed ranks test (Sokal and Rohlf 1969), population differences were examined for statistical significance. For sixteen matched pairs of correlation coefficients (maxillary and mandibular central incisor through third molar), Indian Knoll was more asymmetrical than Campbell/Larson in both the mesiodistal ($p<0.05$) and buccolingual ($p<0.01$) dimensions. When both dimensions were combined, the correlation coefficients of Campbell/Larson exceeded Indian Knoll in twenty-six out of the thirty-two comparisons (Wilcoxon's test, $p< 0.001$). The Hamann group was also significantly less asymmetrical than Indian Knoll. Their r's exceed Indian Knoll in twenty-three out of the thirty-two comparisons (Wilcoxon's test, $p<0.03$). Finally, no significant difference in fluctuating asymmetry could be demonstrated between the Campbell/Larson and Hamann groups. Of interest, too, the author has shown that within the Indian Knoll population, the taller individuals have both significantly larger and less asymmetrical teeth than shorter individuals (Perzigian n.d.).

These results were not unexpected. On the basis of disparate lines of evidence, both archeological and skeletal, the Indian Knoll population was seemingly disadvantaged socioeconomically and nutritionally. Earlier studies (Bailit et al. 1970; DiBennardo 1973) have reported similar associations between the level of dental asymmetry and environmental conditions. Those individuals growing under adverse conditions manifest tendencies not only for asymmetrical teeth, but also for small teeth. Essentially, the same results are reported here, that is, the magnitude of fluctuating asymmetry (*a*) coincides with other indicators of growth disturbance and (*b*) sensitively reflects levels of environmental stress.

Conceivably, genetic factors could explain the differences in asymmetry among the three groups. For example, inbreeding or relaxed natural selection for morphogenetic field integration (Henderson and Greene 1975) might account for the more pronounced asymmetry of Indian Knoll. An inbreeding and asymmetry could be demonstrated for modern Tristanites (Bailit et al. 1970) or Japanese (DiBennardo 1975). In addition, a relaxation of natural selection on the dentition is less likely for a technologically "primitive" population like Indian Knoll than for later, agriculturally based populations such as Campbell and Larson. The most economical explanation, then, lies in the variation in environments among the groups.

The intention here was not to argue that the adoption of agriculture by prehistoric groups resulted, inevitably, in improved living conditions. Many recent authors have, in fact, taken the opposite position (Cassidy 1972; Lallo 1973; Rose 1973; and Robbins in this volume), suggesting that environmental stresses associated with high population density, low protein diet, and exposure to pathogens increased with the abandonment of aboriginal hunting and gathering. Their views seem to be partially influenced by information on the current experiences of many of the people of the nonwestern world, who live under abysmally poor, crowded conditions and consume almost completely vegetarian diets. Recent studies have demonstrated that contemporary hunting and gathering populations have better balanced, nutritious diets and suffer less from infectious disorders than do the world's urban destitute people.

Need we assume, though, that the living conditions during the Middle Mississippi period even remotely parallel those of rural Bangladesh, Guatemala, or Ethiopia? The tendency of some has perhaps been to overestimate the adversities and ills that accompany the prehistoric development of agriculture and underemphasize the effective stresses on hunter-gatherers (Cowgill 1975).

SUMMARY

This paper has presented evidence that data on the size, morphology, and histologic structure of the dentition are valuable sources of information about prehistoric people. Appropriately designed investigations can resolve questions regarding the genetic relationship among populations and contribute to an understanding of their health and nutritional status.

A second contribution made here is to point out that dentition is developmentally plastic and reflects the environmental conditions surrounding the growing organism. When environmental conditions interfere with normal, bilaterally symmetrical morphogenesis, size asymmetries may result. Further supportive evidence is offered to demonstrate that the magnitude of fluctuating dental asymmetry closely corresponds to the level of environmental stress operating on individuals.

The third point made here is that environmental stresses operating during growth were apparently greater on a prehistoric hunting and gathering population than on certain aboriginal farming groups or a modern cadaver sample.

Data presented above tentatively suggest that those groups that successfully developed mixed economies of hunting, gathering, and agriculture suffered less incapacitation during growth than those groups with narrow spectrum economies based exclusively on hunting and gathering. It is hoped that through further studies of dental asymmetry we will more fully understand the biological and adaptive consequences of prehistoric culture change in the New World.

NOTES

1. See Robbins's and Gilbert's findings above. *Editor.*

REFERENCES

Austin, D. M., 1970. *Dental Microevolution in Two Ancient Maya Communities* (M.A. thesis, Pennsylvania State University).

Bader, R. S., 1965. Fluctuating Asymmetry in the Dentition of the House Mouse. *Growth* 29 : 291–300.

Bailit, H. L., 1966. *Tooth Size Variability, Inbreeding, and Evolution.* Annals of the New York Academy of Science, No. 134, pp. 616–623.

———, 1975. Dental Variation Among Populations, An Anthropologic View. *Dental Clinics of North America* 19 : 125–139.

Bailit, H. L., P. L. Workman, J. D. Niswander, and C. J. MacLean, 1970. Dental Asymmetry as an Indicator of Genetic and Environmental Conditions in Human Populations. *Human Biology* 42 : 626–638.

Biggerstaff, R. H., 1975. Cusp Size, Sexual Dimorphism, and Heritability of Cusp Size in Twins. *American Journal of Physical Anthropology* 42 : 127–140.

Brace, C. L., 1967. Environment, Tooth Form, and Size in the Pleistocene. *Journal of Dental Research* 46 : 809–816.

———, n.d. Tooth Reduction in the Orient. *Asian Perspectives.* In press.

Brewer-Carias, C. A., S. LeBlanc, and J. V. Neel, 1976. Genetic Structure of a Tribal Population, the Yanomama Indians. XIII. Dental Microdifferentiation. *American Journal of Physical Anthropology* 44 : 5–14.

Cassidy, C. M., 1972. *Comparison of Nutrition in Pre-agricultural and Ag-*

ricultural Pre-Columbian Skeletal Populations (Ph.D. diss., University of Wisconsin).

Cohen, M. N., 1975. Archaeological Evidence for Population Pressure in Preagricultural Societies. *American Antiquity* 40 : 471–475.

Cook, D. C., 1971. *Patterns of Nutritional Stress in Some Illinois Woodland Populations* (M.A. thesis, University of Chicago).

Cowgill, G. L., 1975. *Population Pressure as a Non-explanation.* Memoirs of the Society for American Archaeology, No. 40, pp. 127–131.

Dahlberg, A. A., 1963. Analysis of the American Indian Dentition. In *Dental Anthropology*, D. R. Brothwell, ed. (New York: Pergamon Press), pp. 149–177.

DiBennardo, R., 1973. *Prenatal Stress, Developmental 'Noise,' and Postnatal Risk* (Ph.D. diss., City University of New York).

DiOrio, L. P., S. A. Miller, and J. M. Navia, 1973. The Separate Effects of Protein and Calorie Malnutrition on the Development and Growth of Rat Bones and Teeth. *Journal of Nutrition* 103 : 856–865.

Ditch, L. E., and J. C. Rose, 1972. A Multivariate Dental Sexing Technique. *American Journal of Physical Anthropology* 37 : 61–64.

Garn, S. M., A. B. Lewis, and A. Walenga, 1968. Evidence for a Secular Trend in Tooth Size Over Two Generations. *Journal of Dental Research* 47 : 503.

Goose, D. H., 1971. The Inheritance of Tooth Size in British Families. In *Dental Morphology and Evolution*, A. A. Dahlberg, ed. (Chicago: University of Chicago Press), pp. 263–270.

Greene, D. L., 1972. Dental Anthropology of Early Egypt and Nubia. *Journal of Human Evolution* 1 : 315–324.

Henderson, A. M., and D. L. Greene, 1975. Dental Field Theory: An Application to Primate Evolution. *Journal of Dental Research* 54 : 344–350.

Hrdlička, A., 1920. Shovel-Shaped Teeth. *American Journal of Physical Anthropology* 3 : 429–465.

Hurt, W. R., 1969. Seasonal Economic and Settlement Patterns of the Arikara. *The Plains Anthropologist* 14 : 32–37.

Hylander, W. L., 1975. Incisor Size and Diet in Anthropoids with Special Reference to Cercopithecidae. *Science* 189 : 1095–1097.

Johnston, F. E., and C. E. Snow, 1961. The Reassessment of the Age and Sex of the Indian Knoll Skeletal Population. *American Journal of Physical Anthropology* 19 : 237–244.

Kapur, K. K., and J. Okubo, 1970. Effect of Impaired Mastication on the Health of Rats. *Journal of Dental Research* 49 : 61–68.

Lallo, J. W., 1973. *The Skeletal Biology of Three Prehistoric American Indian Societies from Dickson Mounds* (Ph.D. diss., University of Massachusetts).

Lavelle, C. L. B., 1970. Analysis of Attrition in Adult Human Molars. *Journal of Dental Research* 49 : 822–828.

LeBlanc, S. A., and B. Black, 1974. A Long Term Trend in Tooth Size in the Eastern Mediterranean. *American Journal of Physical Anthropology* 41 : 417–422.

Lehmer, D. J., and D. T. Jones, 1968. *Arikara Archaeology: The Bad River Phase.* Publications in Salvage Archaeology, No. 7 (Lincoln, Nebr.: Smithsonian Institution, River Basin Surveys).

Lombardi, A. V., 1975. Tooth Size Associations of Three Morphologic Dental Traits in a Melanesian Population. *Journal of Dental Research* 54 : 239–243.

Mayhall, J. R., 1975. Human Dental Morphological Traits: A Change in Adaptive Significance (abstract). *American Journal of Physical Anthropology* 42 : 317.

Molnar, S., 1971. Human Tooth Wear, Tooth Function and Cultural Variability. *American Journal of Physical Anthropology* 34 : 175–189.

———, 1972. Tooth Wear and Culture: A Survey of Tooth Functions Among Some Prehistoric Populations. *Current Anthropology* 13 : 511–526.

Molnar, S., and S. C. Ward, 1975. Mineral Metabolism and Microstructural Defects in Primate Teeth. *American Journal of Physical Anthropology* 43 : 3–18.

Moorrees, C. F. A., 1951. The Dentition as a Criterion of Race with Special Reference to the Aleut. *Journal of Dental Research* 30 : 815–821.

Mumma, R. D., and K. Quinton, 1970. Effect of Masticatory Efficiency on the Occurrence of Gastric Distress. *Journal of Dental Research* 49 : 69–74.

Parmalee, P. W., and W. E. Klippel, 1974. Freshwater Mussels as a Prehistoric Food Source. *American Antiquity* 39 : 421–434.

Paynter, K. J., and R. M. Grainger, 1956. The Relation of Nutrition to the Morphology and Size of Rat Molar Teeth. *Journal of the Canadian Dental Association* 22 : 519–531.

Perzigian, A. J., 1975. Natural Selection on the Dentition of an Arikara Population. *American Journal of Physical Anthropology* 42 : 63–70.

———, n.d. Fluctuating Dental Asymmetry: Variation among Skeletal Populations. (Manuscript in preparation, Department of Anthropology, University of Cincinnati.)

Rose, J., 1973. *Analysis of Dental Microdefects of Prehistoric Populations from Illinois* (Ph.D. diss., University of Massachusetts).

Rosenzweig, K. A., and P. Smith, 1971. Dental Variability in Isolates. *Journal of Dental Research* 50 : 155–160.

Sciulli, P. W., and R. Carlisle, 1975. Analysis of the Dentition from Three Western Pennsylvania Late Woodland Sites. I. Descriptive Statistics, Partition of Variation and Asymmetry. *Pennsylvania Archaeologist* 45 : 47–54.

Scott, E. C., 1974. *Dental Variation in Pre-Columbian Coastal Peru* (Ph.D. diss., University of Missouri).

Shkurkin, G. V., A. J. Almquist, A. A. Pfeihofer, and E. L. Stoddard, 1975. Scanning Electron Microscopy of Dentition: Methodology and Ultrastructural Morphology of Tooth Wear. *Journal of Dental Research* 54 : 402–406.

Siegel, M. I., and W. J. Doyle, 1975. The Differential Effects of Prenatal and Postnatal Audiogenic Stress on Fluctuating Dental Asymmetry. *Journal of Experimental Zoology* 191 : 211–214.

Smith, B. D., 1974. Middle Mississippi Exploitation of Animal Populations: A Predictive Model. *American Antiquity* 39 : 274–291.

Smith, P., 1973. Variations in Dental Traits Within Populations. (Paper presented at the 9th International Congress of Anthropological and Ethnological Sciences, Inc., Chicago.)

Snyder, R. G., A. A. Dahlberg, C. C. Snow, and T. Dahlberg, 1969. Trait Analysis of the Dentition of the Tarahumara Indians and Mestizos of the Sierra Madre, Occidental, Mexico. *American Journal of Physical Anthropology* 31 : 65–76.

Sofaer, J. A., J. D. Niswander, J. D. MacLean, and P. L. Workman, 1972. Population Studies on Southwestern Indian Tribes. V. Tooth Morphology as an Indicator of Biological Distance. *American Journal of Physical Anthropology* 37 : 357–366.

Sognnaes, R. F., 1956. Histologic Evidence of Developmental Lesions in Teeth Originating from Palaeolithic, Prehistoric and Ancient Man. *American Journal of Pathology* 32 : 547–577.

Sokal, R. R., and F. J. Rohlf, 1969. *Biometry* (San Francisco: Freeman).

Suarez, B. K., 1974. Neanderthal Dental Asymmetry and the Probable Mutation Effect. *American Journal of Physical Anthropology* 41 : 411–416.

Tenczar, P., and R. S. Bader, 1966. Maternal Effect in Dental Traits of the House Mouse. *Science* 152 : 1398–1400.

Turner, C. G., 1967. Dental Genetics and Microevolution in Prehistoric and Living Koniag Eskimo. *Journal of Dental Research* 46 : 911–917.

————, 1971. Three-rooted Mandibular First Permanent Molars and the Question of American Indian Origins. *American Journal of Physical Anthropology* 34 : 229–242.

Van Valen, L., 1962. A Study of Fluctuating Asymmetry. *Evolution* 16 : 125–142.

Wedel, W. R., 1961. *Prehistoric Man on the Great Plains* (Norman: University of Oklahoma Press).

Winters, H. D., 1969. *The Riverton Culture*. Reports of Investigations, No. 13 (Springfield: Illinois State Museum).

————, 1974. Introduction to the New Edition. In *Indian Knoll*, by W. S. Webb. (Knoxville: University of Tennessee Press), pp. v–xxvii.

Wolpoff, M. H., 1971. Interstitial Wear. *American Journal of Physical Anthropology* 34 : 205–225.

Biocultural Adaptation in Prehistoric America: An Archeologist's Perspective

CHRISTOPHER S. PEEBLES

We can never be in the past; it is only a spectacle before us which is there for us to question. The questions come from us, and thus the responses in principle do not exhaust historical reality, since historical reality does not depend upon them for its existence.—Merleau-Ponty (1964:194).

THE six substantive papers that form the core of this volume draw attention to the fact that the paths to knowledge about the human past are manifold and complex. These papers demonstrate the value of asking new questions and, for that matter, asking old questions in new ways. The papers demonstrate, both separately and as a unit, that the biological components of archeological data—both those already excavated and those that remain in the ground—can if properly questioned add markedly to our knowledge of both the biological and cultural dimensions of past human populations. Access to this knowledge, however, is not to be gained without additional effort beyond previous attempts. The variety of successful methods and procedures described in these papers demands that archeologists extend their excavation techniques to recover adequate samples of data for such analyses. Conversely, it is incumbent upon physical anthropologists to aid the archeologist in the recognition and recovery of these data, and in addition to be conversant with archeological methods, techniques, and results. It is evident from these papers that such extra effort will be repaid many times over, and both biological and cultural anthropology will be the richer.

From the perspective of an archeologist, the methods, techniques, and results presented in these papers fall into two broad areas. First, they extend and amplify our perception of what kinds of biological data must be collected from an excavation. They give us, by virtue of this recognition, access to some aspects of human behavior that are mirrored poorly, if at all, in the artifactual record. Second, the results of the analyses reported here provide evidence that either supports or calls into question models and explanations of cultural stability and change currently held by archeologists.

The notion of stasis and evolution of biological and cultural systems introduces the concept of adaptation. Human populations, like all other living systems, adapt to a natural environment; but, unlike other living systems, they effect this adaptation through both somatic (genetic) and extrasomatic (cultural) means. In principle, however, the strategy of adaptation—even with the addition of a cultural system—is similar for both human and nonhuman populations. As Slobodkin and Rapoport (1974) argue, all living systems play a game of Gamblers Ruin with their environments. To lose such a game is to become extinct; to win such a game is not possible, because the organism cannot pick up its chips and leave. To stay in the game is the only goal. The optimal strategy to stay in a game of Gamblers Ruin is to constantly minimize the risks associated with playing the game. Responses to perturbations in the environment, which are equal to plays of the game, should be organized as a multilinked combination of hierarchical and direct communication pathways. Such a system can move to counteract the fluctuation and at the same time maintain sufficient flexibility to deal with simultaneous or subsequent perturbations.

> . . . successful evolution requires the maintenance of flexibility in response to environmental perturbation and this flexibility must be maintained in the most parsimonious way. The parsimony argument is that organisms must not make an excessive or unnecessary commitment in responding to perturbation, but at the same time the deeper responses must be ready to take over to the degree that the superficial responses are ineffective. This effect would seem most simply achieved if the environmental perturbation started responses on all levels simultaneously and, to the degree that the rapid and superficial response mechanisms succeeded in restoring the organism to its preperturbation state, the deeper levels have not had time to react very strongly before the stimulus for the reaction has disappeared. (Slobodkin and Rapoport 1974:198).

A system behaving in this manner affects only the minimum response necessary (or possible) to counteract the perturbation. It avoids the deeper, higher stakes responses and the higher probability that a single unfavorable outcome will end the game.

For human populations, like other species, perturbations in the environment can be met through their biological systems in several ways. In order of increasing expense, permanence, inclusiveness, and risk, these responses include: (*a*) changes in individual behavior; (*b*) changes in individual physiology; (*c*) changes in individual physiological acclimatization; (*d*) changes in the death rate of individuals within a population; (*e*) selective fecundity and mortality within a population; and finally (*f*) deep genetic changes that affect anatomy, innate behavior, and other aspects of the population as a whole (Slobodkin and Rapoport 1974: fig. 1; Bateson 1963).

Adaptive responses for human populations can also come from the cultural system. The order and risk of responses in this system likewise can be arranged in order of cost. Such responses can be as minimal as changes in individual behavior or the behavior of local groups; at a slightly more costly level minor changes in exploitive technology can be incorporated and small shifts in organization can be effected; finally, there can be changes in the totality of a cultural system's energy base, organization, and symbolic representations. Changes in the biological system of human populations can select for changes in the cultural system and changes in the cultural system can select for changes in the population's biological system. That is, each forms part of the environment for the other. Moreover, biology and culture together are matched against the environment. Either they are successful together and the game goes on or they are unsuccessful and the game comes closer to the end.

Archeologists are able to measure some changes in the cultural systems they study. These papers, however, point the way to analyzing much finer variation within the biological systems of prehistoric populations and perhaps give us additional ways to measure change in cultural systems. As Perzigian shows, teeth are very sensitive indicators of many aspects of human behavior. Teeth reflect diet, food-preparation techniques, and their use as tools; teeth can be used as an indicator of the age and sex of an individual within a population; and teeth reflect genetic distance between populations and genetic change within sequent populations through time. Robbins points out that dental pathology and attrition reflect the state of health of a population and individual compensatory behavior in response to dental pathology. She also sketches a variety of other biocultural data preserved in the archeological record that reflect individual responses to fluctuations in the environment.

Gilbert's paper demonstrates the power and sensitivity—as well as the pitfalls—of trace element analysis of human bone. Not only can trace element analysis indicate the approximate position of a population in the food chain, but it can also reflect differential access to foodstuffs by individuals and socially defined groups. Robbins gives a sketch of how trace element analysis can be used to analyze the effects on Late Woodland populations in Kentucky of soils and a biome woefully deficient in certain essential mineral nutrients. These papers show that—given a proper sample, good control over factors affecting the inclusion (*in vivo*) and destruction (*in vitro*) of trace elements, and good laboratory techniques —trace element analysis can be used to assess the health of a population and the relationship of a population to its food resources.

These and other analytical techniques, the measurement of population dynamics and the assessment of genetic distance between populations, for example, all demand greater cooperation between physical anthropologists and archeologists. Such cooperation must include collaboration both in construction of the research design and in execution of the research design in the field. Standard archeological field techniques, as Robbins demonstrates, fail to recognize many pieces of bone as human. At Indian Knoll, for instance, fetal elements were catalogued as animal rather than human bone; and at Moundville I discovered a third, unpublished achondroplastic dwarf classified as an "unknown" animal (cf. Snow 1943). Moreover, the very act of excavation, no matter how careful it may be, destroys many of the smaller skeletal elements. These small pieces, if perceived during excavation, can be measured and analyzed *in situ*. Additionally, Robbins directs attention to microfloral and microfaunal materials in the grave fill. If these data are systematically collected, the season of interment and the stomach contents of the corpse might be ascertained.

The major methodological prescription offered to archeologists by these papers is the necessity to include biological anthropologists (and their special knowledge) as active participants in all phases of archeological research. The papers by Buikstra and Robbins are excellent examples of how biological anthropologists and archeologists together can accomplish more than either can separately. As Buikstra's paper points out, the methods used to guide the research in the lower Illinois Valley grew from the recognition that cultural and biological variability were conceptually and empirically interrelated, not only with each other, but also with the environment as a whole. To maximize the data recovered from each excavation, therefore, cooperation between anthropologists of various specialties as well as that of other scientists had to be incorporated into the project as a whole. This collaboration was not of the "get a natural scientist to do the ————" (here fill in the blank with soils, skeletons, sherds, etc.) after the materials have been excavated. Instead, the special sampling and recovery requirements for the several classes of data were included in the research design. The accomplishments of the mortuary survey and excavations reported by Buikstra are sufficient justification for the adoption of such research methods.

In addition to presenting technical and methodological aspects of biological anthropology, five of these six papers address major problems in the evolution and organization of cultural systems. The substantive results given here either add to or call into question models that are used currently to represent the prehistory of the eastern United States. The disparate analyses reported here touch on the nutritional and demographic status of hunter-gatherer groups (Buikstra, Perzigian, Robbins), the adoption of agriculture (Buikstra, Robbins), and the origins and organization of the Mississippian period (Blakely, Wolf). It is to these topics that I will now turn.

THE ORIGINAL AFFLUENT SOCIETY

In recent years the anthropological view of hunter-gatherer populations has changed radically. In textbooks and monographs published before 1950, hunter-gatherers were cast in a Hobbesian mold: in brief their life was "solitary, poor, nasty, brutish, and short." In the 1960's, following Lee's work with the Bushmen (Lee 1965), hunter-gatherers were pictured as people of limited wants and unlimited means who, as good ecologists, kept their populations well below the carrying capacity of their environment. Sahlins (1972) has characterized these hunter-gatherer groups as "the original affluent society." He says, "Hunters and gatherers have by force of circumstances an objectively low standard of living. But taken as their *objective*, and given their adequate means of production, all the people's material wants usually can be easily satisfied" (Sahlins 1972:36–37). Archeologists are incorporating Sahlins' neo-Rousseauian view of the noble, well-provisioned, happy hunter-gatherer into their models and explanations. For example, Caldwell, who was in a few ways ahead of his time, summed up the preagricultural prehistory of the eastern United States in three words: "primary forest efficiency" (Caldwell 1958). He believed that the Archaic and Early Woodland populations of the eastern woodlands were so well adapted to their habitat that they actively resisted all changes, especially the introduction of agriculture.

Like all polar opposites and ideal types, the concepts of the original affluent society and the hungry hunter-gatherer each contain some truth, but neither is wholly correct. Two of the papers in this volume present data that demonstrate dietary stress in hunter-gatherer populations and thereby call for judicious use of Sahlins' model and Caldwell's conclusions. Perzigian analyzes the asymmetric development of teeth (which is a stress indicator) in hunter-gatherer, prehistoric agricultural, and modern populations. His analysis shows that when compared to the other two groups, the development of the dentition among hunter-gatherers shows greater stress during growth and development. Buikstra outlines a number of lines of evidence that suggest that Middle Woodland populations, which may have been part-time horticulturalists, were subjected to acute, episodic stress. Robbins' work with the Indian Knoll and Carlson Annis shellmound Archaic materials should produce similar results. As she points out, the extreme robusticity and lack of sexual dimorphism in the Carlson Annis population certainly suggests a strenuous life.

AGRICULTURE: BOON OR BLIGHT?

The adoption of agriculture was, as Flannery emphasizes, a process and not an event (Flannery 1973). The path to food production involved preadaptations in the form of tools, processing and storage techniques, and in the domesticants themselves. Agriculture itself was the product of many small changes in cultural systems that were fixed by positive feed-back. In addition, agriculture was itself the cause of many changes in the biological system of humans and in their ecosystem. Flannery has argued recently that a single model—such as population pressure—will not subsume all occurrences in which agriculture has been adopted (Flannery 1973 : 307). That is, he does not believe that there is a single "prime mover" that selects for an agricultural way of life. However, Flannery does characterize the situation in which agriculture must have seemed an attractive alternative: "Since early farming represents a deci-sion to work harder and to eat more 'third-choice' foods, I suspect that the people did it because they felt they *had* to, not because they wanted to" (Flannery 1973 : 307–308). In brief, although the situation for the selection of agriculture may have varied in content (state of the system variables) from place to place and time to time, the evidence does sug-gest that the aggregate pressure for the selection for this mode of pro-duction must have been acute.

In the eastern United States there were two sequential and related epi-sodes during which crops were brought under effective domestication. The first, earlier episode (ca. 1000 B.C.) involved the "Eastern Agricul-tural Complex" of cultigens native to the eastern woodlands (Struever and Vickery 1973; Ford 1974); the second, later episode (ca. A.D. 400) incorporated the tropical cultigens, especially maize and later beans, into the agricultural regime (Ford 1974). The papers by Buikstra and Rob-bins untangle some of the causal linkages and consequences associated with the adoption of agriculture in the eastern woodlands.

Buikstra's paper, despite the fact that it is a report of work still in progress, is nevertheless the most inclusive and sophisticated exposition to date of the changes in biological and cultural variables prior to, during, and after the shift to maize agriculture. Following Ford (1974), she argues that the major benefit of maize agriculture is that it provides a buffer against seasonal privation and random fluctuations in the environment: that is, maize is a high-yield, storable crop and as such can be used to dampen fluctuations in the abundance of other foodstuffs. The situation preceding the adoption of maize in the lower Illinois Valley seems to have included acute episodic stress, an increasing population, shrinking collecting territories, and, at least in the early Late Woodland, the appearance of warfare. Following the incorporation of maize into the subsistence cycle, the population continues to increase, mortality increases for adolescents and young adults, social complexity increases, and chronic stress is substituted for acute, episodic stress.

Although population density does play a role in the systemic model developed by Buikstra, neither it nor any other variable in her model can be assigned the role of a "prime mover." Instead there is a complicated (and probably incomplete) multicausal network of variables. I might add that whatever systemic stability was attained in the Middle Woodland period of the lower Illinois Valley, it was exchanged during the Late Woodland period for a series of deviation amplification loops that ended in a period of devolution at a point in time subsequent to the Mississippi period but before European contact.

Robbins' analysis of the Fort Ancient agricultural populations, like Buikstra's, represents a major work that is still in progress. Moreover, her results provide a marked contrast when compared to Buikstra's lower Illinois Valley agricultural populations. At the Buckner site, which is located in the truly marginal habitat of the Inner Blue Grass region of Kentucky, Robbins shows that the resident population was subjected to major and unyielding dietary stress and chronic and degenerative diseases. Life at this site must have been truly Hobbesian in nature. Because the Buckner site and other Fort Ancient components in this region represent an immigrant population that invaded an essentially unoccupied niche, one can speculate about the conditions they left in their homeland. Robbins' work on infanticide and population dynamics at the Incinerator site, which is in the Fort Ancient heartland, may provide answers to this question.

MISSISSIPPIAN SOCIETIES

The term *Mississippian* is applied to the final prehistoric epoch of cultural development in the southeastern United States; the cultural systems that evolved during this period represented the most complex native

American societies north of Mexico. Although Mississippian cultural systems depended on hunting for a significant part of their diet, the majority of their foodstuffs came from agricultural crops, especially maize. In fact Griffin (1967 : 189) uses the term Mississippian to characterize "the wide variety of adaptations made by societies which developed a dependence upon agriculture for their basic, storable food supply." The dependence on agriculture can be recognized among societies in the central and lower Mississippi Valley at approximately A.D. 700. Slightly later, at approximately A.D. 900, Early Mississippian systems are present in eastern Tennessee and central Alabama, as well as in other parts of the Southeast. There seems to be direct, *in situ* evolutionary development between the several local manifestations of early Mississippian culture systems and their later mature Mississippian counterparts. Cultural systems of the period A.D. 1100–1500, represented by sites such as Cahokia, Spiro, Moundville, and Etowah, have local, Early Mississippian ancestors.

Although Wolf's paper misrepresents the current state of the archeology of Mississippian societies, the results of his analysis of genetic distance between several Mississippian populations underscores the local development of these societies. He concludes, as have archeologists for several years, that migrations and invasions need not be invoked to account for this phenomenon called the Mississippian.

Wolf's summary presentation of the "results of almost a century of Mississippian archeology" highlights the need for greater cooperation between biological anthropologists and archeologists. Examples include the following:

1. Etowah and the early Mississippian occupation at Macon Plateau are separated by 120 miles and at least 200 years.

2. Most archeologists do not consider the Central Mississippi River Valley the heart from which Mississippian populations and society radiated. Recent work by Faulkner (1974) in Tennessee, Jenkins (Jenkins and Nielsen 1974) in Alabama, Brown (1975) in Oklahoma, and many others points to indigenous development of the several Mississippian cultures in their respective areas.

3. In addition to the historic ties between the Shawnee and Fort Ancient and the Fatherland site with the Natchez, ties have been established between the Fuller Cemetery and the Chickasaw by Nash (Griffin, personal communication), Menard and other lower Mississippi Valley sites with the Quapaw (Phillips, Ford, and Griffin 1951; Phillips 1970), various sites in the Yazoo Basin with the Tunica (Brain, personal communication) and additional sites in the lower Mississippi Valley with the De Soto expedition (Brain, Toth, and Buckingham 1974).

4. The vast majority of the skeletal material excavated from Mississippian and other sites in the southeast, contrary to Wolf's suggestion otherwise, has been saved. There are, for example, over 10,000 burials from Alabama, Mississippi, and Tennessee stored at Mound State Monument, Alabama. These skeletons are well documented, well curated, and ready for study. Moreover, almost 1,000 of these skeletons are from Moundville.

5. There is a site report for the excavations at Moundville; although it is presently in press, the manuscript has been available for seven years (Peebles, n.d.).

6. Finally, in the absence of analysis, the assertion that the skeletons in his sample all represent "similar social classes" is problematical at best and misleading at worst.

Wolf is correct, however, in asserting that the analysis of skeletal materials in the Southeast has fallen far behind conceptual advances in biological anthropology. An analysis similar to the one he presents here should be carried out on a large sample of Mississippian populations so that a map of phenotypic distances could be compared to maps of geographical and cultural distances.

The paper by Blakely demonstrates the impressive amount of information contained in the skeletal material excavated from the major Mississippian center of Etowah. In contrast to the Fort Ancient agriculturalists, the Mississippian population at Etowah seems to have been well provisioned. At Etowah a relatively high population density was maintained, and once an individual passed into late childhood, if warfare and sacrifice did not intervene, a full life span could be anticipated. The demographic profile Blakely constructs for the Etowah site as a whole and the contrast between the age profiles of the mound and village cemetery are similar to those at Moundville (Peebles 1974). However, in the absence of the archeological data for Mound C, Blakely's cultural interpretation of the contrast between mound and village is incomplete.

He argues that the mere fact of being interred in the mound is indicative of superordinate status and, by implication, that all burials in the mound are of equal status. The assumption of equal status for all mound burials is unjustified, as a perusal of Morehead's report (1932) on his mound C excavations will demonstrate. As at Moundville, there are a number of distinct burial programs and statuses represented in Mound C at Etowah. These burials range in rank from "retainer" sacrifices and trophy skulls to the penultimate status represented by burial 57 reported by Larson (1971). Therefore, the test for ranking that I have suggested (Peebles 1974; Peebles and Kus n.d.) cannot be applied to these burials until their cultural variables are analyzed. Moreover, I did not suggest that the model of ranked societies I used was either inflexible or univariate. Within this class called chiefdoms there is a wide range of organizational complexity. There is no ideal type of chiefdom. There is only a class labeled chiefdom for which Kus and I have suggested some archeologically visible correlates (see below).

Given a model of a ranked society, biological consequences can, however, be predicted. If a ramage or conical clan is assumed and some marriage rules can be postulated, then coefficients of consanguinity, relationship, and inbreeding can be calculated. These simulated data can then be matched with phenotypic distances between individuals, and socially defined classes of individuals within the population. Blakely's discriminant analysis of craniometric variables for the Etowah population although not "statistically significant" does suggest that Mound C females are phenotypically distinct from the remainder of the population. These results would be consistent with a conical clan in which descent, succession, and filiation were matrilineal, in which class exogomy was enforced, and where females of the highest ranking lineage were proportionately overrepresented in the mound. That is, these results "fit," albeit loosely, with the model of Natchez social organization developed by White, Murdock, and Scaglion (1971). In summary, I can only say that I wish Blakely had worked on the Moundville skeletal materials. If he had, my analysis of the cultural dimensions of mortuary practices would have been far more complete.

BURIALS AND THE ANALYSIS OF SOCIAL ORGANIZATION

A human burial contains more anthropological information per cubic meter of deposit than any other type of archeological feature. A burial represents the latent images of a biological and cultural person frozen in a clearly delimited segment of space and time. Analysis of these human remains by physical anthropologists can yield measures of the age, sex, physical abilities, history of diet and disease, and sometimes, the cause of death of the individual. Archeologists can analyze the content of the burial, the grave goods, and the grave fill and reconstruct the sequence of acts and items that composed the mortuary ritual that created the interment. If there is an adequate sample of burials from a locality or a region, and if the archeological control of these features is sufficiently precise, then these burials can be used to construct demographic and social models for either a community or for an entire cultural system.

All the papers in this volume discuss aspects of the analysis of biological variables of individual burials and seek to relate these measures to prehistoric populations. Several of these papers discuss the social and cultural correlates of the biological variability observed in prehistoric populations. I would like to pick up this latter theme and briefly discuss some recent work by archeologists on the cultural dimensions of mortuary ritual.

Most recent analyses of mortuary ritual have taken their impetus from one or more of the papers given in a symposium entitled "Approaches to the Social Dimensions of Mortuary Practices" (Brown, ed. 1971) given at the 1966 meeting of the Society for American Archaeology. In the key paper of this symposium Binford argued that there are systematic, observable relationships between social organization and the organization of mortuary ritual. He showed (with the aid of a small sample of ethnographic cases) that the social persona of the deceased (the sum of statuses and identity relationships of the deceased [see Goodenough 1965]) was reflected in the mortuary ritual. In addition, Binford demonstrated that the number of social personae covaried with social complexity; therefore the complexity of burial structure and organization as measured archeologically should covary with societal complexity (Binford 1971 : 23). That is, each individual has a "status in death," and that individual's mortuary ritual reflects the reciprocal rights and duties called forth by this status with respect to the wider society. Burials, therefore, could be used to measure the organizational complexity of society.

The initial postulates put forward by Binford were expanded, cast as a series of eight specific hypotheses, and tested in depth with ethnographic data from three societies by Saxe (Saxe 1970). Saxe began with Binford's hypotheses that variability in burial organization reflected variability in social personae, and that this variability was congruent with the organizing principles of the society as a whole. He proposed as an auxiliary hypothesis that the aspects of a social persona that reflected higher rank would take precedence over lower ranking aspects in the organization of mortuary ceremonialism. For example, the identity relationship engendered by the status of king would take precedence over those of father or spouse or clan chief. He proposed componential and information-theoretic measures of burial complexity that would also serve as indirect measures of societal complexity. He next proposed that the more complex the society, the greater the difference would be accorded "deviant" individuals in mortuary ritual. Finally he put forward the hypothesis that the greater the control by lineal descent groups over scarce or strategic resources, the more probable that such a group would maintain a corporate area for the disposal of their dead. Saxe tested these hypotheses and measures with ethnographic data from the Ashanti, the Kapauku Papuans, and the Bontoc Igorot. In general all but one of the hypotheses withstood the test. One of the componential measures failed completely. Although Saxe specifically warned that his work was not to be used as a "cookbook" for the analysis of archeological data, it has served as a major source of ideas and support for such analyses.

The methods, measures, and techniques for the analysis of prehistoric disposal domains, mortuary ritual, and social personae are only now being developed. Two analytical constraints, however, are already evident from the projects that have been completed. First, it is necessary to work with an adequate sample of burials that proportionately represent all disposal types practiced by the society. The analysis of burial organization, regardless of the algorithm or strategy chosen, proceeds by the comparison and contrast of distinctive features of mortuary ritual. In fact, such analyses are much like phonemic analysis in linguistics. If major segments of the burial population are missing, then any definition of social personae and any model of social organization constructed from these personae will be incorrect. Second, the measures used to analyze prehistoric disposal domains will differ qualitatively between societies. Items, acts, and symbols used to mark differences in one society may be a matter of indifference to members of another society. There are measures that can be used to analyze disposal domains both within and between societies, but the exclusive use of these measures may mask significant variety observable within a single disposal domain.

Tainter (1973) has suggested that variability in the amount of energy expended on mortuary ritual is the best measure for the analysis of disposal domains both within and between societies. He begins with Binford's argument that death calls forth the full array of relationships between the social personae of the deceased and society at large. The higher the rank of the deceased, the greater the number of relationships, the greater the corporate involvement, therefore the greater the amount of energy expended in the mortuary ritual. In addition, Tainter (1975) has used several sociological measures of bureaucracy to analyze prehistoric social organization. He used these several measures to analyze the changes in social organization that took place between the Middle Woodland and Late Woodland periods in the lower Illinois Valley (cf., Buikstra, this volume).

Rothschild used the technical measure of "information" to analyze changes in social organization in the eastern United States (Rothschild 1975). Specifically, she used information-theoretic measures of diversity, evenness, and redundancy to assess changing age and sex roles as manifested in burials from the Archaic through Mississippian periods. She found that as social complexity increased, the number of social personae reflected in the several burial populations multiplied, and social personae became much more rigidly defined in terms of this mortuary ritual.

One of the major areas of concern in the analysis of prehistoric disposal domains has been in the identification of ranking and the rise of chiefdoms. Such societies are not only interesting in their own right, but some chiefdoms (what could be termed complex chiefdoms to separate them from "big men" societies) later went on to become states. In a paper to be published in the near future Kus and I suggest an unambiguous test for the presence of a ranked society as reflected in the organization of burials. Because Blakely (this volume) uses this test in his analysis of the Etowah population, I have included it below:

> The test for ranking is not merely the presence of richly accompanied child or infant burials. A test for ranking based on the mortuary ceremonialism of an archaeologically defined society must confirm the prediction of two clear, independent dimensions of social personae represented in the burials. The first, *ascribed dimension*, must be a partial ordering which is based on symbols, energy expenditure, and other variables of mortuary ritual, and which is *not* simultaneously ordered on the basis of age and sex. In the ascribed dimension some infants, some children, and some adults will be found in every scale category except the paramount category. This apical class will contain only adults, and probably only adult males. That is, in the ascribed dimension some infants and children will be ranked equally with some adults and higher than other adults in a lower scale position. Some infants and children will have greater amounts of energy expended on their mortuary ritual than some adults; in the same manner some women will be ranked higher than some men and will share status-specific symbols with some men.
>
> The second, *achieved dimension* will be a partial order based on symbols, energy expenditure and other variables, which generally will be ordered on the basis of age and sex. In the achieved dimension, as the chronological age of the burial increases so will the energy expended on that individual's burial: adult burials will be more complex and evince greater energy expenditure than those of children; child burials will be more complex and evince greater energy expenditure than those of infants. Children and infants will have some items as grave goods that will not be shared by adults; women will have some items as grave goods not shared by men. In general, the symbols of rank and office (Binford's sociotechnic artifacts) of the ascribed dimension will not be found in the achieved dimension. In addition, the energy expended for the lowest ranking burials in the ascribed dimension will be higher than that expended on the highest ranking burials of the achieved dimension. Lastly, the numbers of burials in each scale category in the ascribed dimension should decrease markedly as one goes higher on the scale, thereby reflecting the ranking pyramid. The numbers of individuals in each scale category of

the achieved dimension should reflect the age and sex pyramid of the population through time (Peebles and Kus n.d. : 25; see also Peebles 1974).

There have been several analyses of Mississippi period cultural systems in the eastern United States that have demonstrated a ranked form of organization for these societies. My work with the Moundville Phase in Alabama has begun to unravel the organization of this major ceremonial center and its relationships with other sites that make up the Moundville Phase (Peebles 1971, 1972, 1974, n.d.). Hatch has presented an extended analysis of the burial organization of the Dallas Phase in Tennessee and has demonstrated a ranked form of organization for this society (Hatch 1974; Hatch and Willey 1974). Larson has argued that the Middle Mississippi settlement at Etowah, Georgia, represented the remains of a stratified society (Larson 1971; see also Blakely, this volume). Brown has presented a masterful set of analyses of the very complex, ranked organization manifested in the burials at Spiro, Oklahoma (Brown 1966a, 1966b, 1971, 1975). Finally, Goldstein has shown that in the lower Illinois Valley local communities, which themselves are part of a ranked society, evince egalitarian internal organization (Goldstein 1976).

The above analyses all depend to a greater or lesser extent on the talents of physical anthropologists. Social organization is embroidered on a tapestry of age, sex, and ability. Accurate assessments of these variables provide the basic background dimensions for the analysis of mortuary ceremonialism. If social ranking is present, then it cross cuts age and sex lines within a segment of society. If corporate groups bury their dead together, then assessment of epigenetic traits should buttress observed similarities in mortuary ritual. If warfare is endemic and death in battle is marked by special mortuary treatment, then physical anthropologists must provide the archeologist with the indications of such a death. Finally, physical anthropologists can provide archeologists with data necessary to assess the adequacy of their sample of burials. If the ages and sexes of the sample being analyzed fit no known distribution, then it is incumbent on the physical anthropologist to tell the archeologist that he or she has real problems, that part of the population is missing.

In conclusion, I would like to again pick up the theme that runs through all these papers—that of cooperation and collaboration between biological anthropologists and archeologists. If archeologists seek explanations for variability in cultural systems, then these explanations must be phrased in terms of that system's environment. The immediate environment of a cultural system is that of the human biological system. Once these two systems are conjoined into a biocultural system, then the natural environment becomes the selective milieu in which human groups exist. Therefore, parochialism in either method, theory, or technique by either biological or cultural anthropologists will be productive only of bad science. Cooperation is not only necessary, but, as these papers demonstrate, it is extremely fruitful.

REFERENCES

Bateson, G., 1963. The Role of Scientific Change in Evolution. *Evolution* 17 : 529–539.

Binford, L., 1971. Mortuary Practices: Their Study and Their Potential. In *Approaches to the Study of Mortuary Practices*, J. Brown, ed. Memoir 25, Society for American Archaeology, pp. 6–29.

Brain, J. P., A. Toth, and A. Rodriguez-Buckingham, 1972. Ethnohistoric Archaeology and the DeSoto Entrada into the Lower Mississippi Valley. *Conference on Historic Site Archaeology Papers* 7 : 232–289.

Brown, J., 1966a. *Spiro Studies: Description of the Mound Group* (Norman, Okla.: Stovall Museum).

————, 1966b. *Spiro Studies: The Graves and Their Contents* (Norman, Okla.: Stovall Museum).

————, 1971. The Dimensions of Status in the Burials at Spiro. In *Approaches to the Social Dimensions of Mortuary Practices*, Memoir 25, Society for American Archaeology.

Faulkner, C., 1974. The Mississippian-Woodland Transition in the East Tennessee Valley. (Paper read at the 31st Southeastern Archaeological Conference, Atlanta.)

Flannery, K., 1973. The Origins of Agriculture. *Annual Review of Anthropology* 2 : 271–310.

Ford, R., 1974. Northeastern Archaeology: Past and Future Directions. *Annual Review of Anthropology* 4 : 385–414.

Goldstein, L., 1976. *Spatial Structure and Social Organization: Regional Manifestations of Mississippian Society* (Ph.D. diss., Northwestern University).

Goodenough, W., 1965. Rethinking 'Status' and 'Role': Toward a General Model of the Cultural Organization of Social Relationships. In *The Relevance of Models for Social Anthropology*, M. Banton, ed. (London, Tavistock), pp. 1–24.

Griffin, J., 1967. Eastern North American Archaeology: A Summary. *Science* 156 : 175–191.

Hatch, J., 1974. *Social Dimensions of Dallas Mortuary Patterns* (M.A. thesis, Pennsylvania State University).

Hatch, J., and P. Willey, 1974. Stature and Status in Dallas Society. *Tennessee Archaeologist* 30 : 107–131.

Jenkins, N., and J. Nielsen, 1974. *Archaeological Salvage Investigations at the West Jefferson Steam Plant Site, Jefferson County, Alabama* (University, Ala.: Department of Anthropology, University of Alabama).

130   *Biocultural Adaptation in Prehistoric America*

Larson, L., Jr., 1971. Archaeological Implications of Social Stratification at the Etowah Site, Georgia. In *Approaches to the Social Dimensions of Mortuary Practices*, J. Brown, ed. Memoir 25, Society for American Archaeology, pp. 58–67.

Lee, R., 1965. *Subsistence Ecology of !Kung Bushmen* (Ph.D. diss., University of California, Berkeley).

Merleau-Ponty, M., 1964. *The Primacy of Perception* (Evanston, Ill.: Northwestern University Press).

Moorehead, W., 1932. *The Etowah Papers* (Andover, Mass.: Phillips Academy; New Haven: Yale University Press).

Peebles, C., 1971. Moundville and Surrounding Sites: Some Structural Considerations of Mortuary Practices. In *Approaches to the Social Dimensions of Mortuary Practices*, J. Brown, ed. Memoir 25, Society for American Archaeology, pp. 68–95.

————, 1972. Monothetic-Divisive Analysis of the Moundville Burials. *Newsletter of Computer Archaeology* 8(2) : 1–13.

————, 1974. *Moundville: The Organization of a Prehistoric Community and Culture* (Ph.D. diss., University of California, Santa Barbara).

————, n.d. *Excavations at Moundville: 1905–1951. Bulletin of the Alabama Museum of Natural History*. In press.

Peebles, C., and S. Kus, n.d. Some Archaeological Correlates of Ranked Societies. (Manuscript, Museum of Anthropology, University of Michigan.)

Phillips, Philip, 1970. *Archaeological Survey in the Lower Yazoo Basin, Mississippi, 1949–1955*. Papers of the Peabody Museum of Archaeology and Ethnology, No. 60, Parts 1 and 2 (Cambridge, Mass.: Peabody Museum).

Phillips, P., J. A. Ford, and J. B. Griffin, 1951. *Archaeological Survey in the Lower Mississippi Alluvial Valley*. Papers of the Peabody Museum of Archaeology and Ethnology, No. 25 (Cambridge, Mass.: Peabody Museum).

Rothschild, N., 1975. *Age and Sex, Status and Role, in Prehistoric Societies of Eastern North America* (Ph.D. diss., New York University).

Sahlins, M., 1972. *Stone Age Economics* (Chicago: Aldine).

Saxe, Arthur, 1970. *Social Dimensions of Mortuary Practices* (Ph.D. diss., University of Michigan).

Slobodkin, L., and A. Rapoport, 1974. An Optimal Strategy of Evolution. *Quarterly Review of Biology* 49 : 181–200.

Snow, C., 1943. *Two Prehistoric Indian Dwarf Skeletons from Moundville*. Museum Paper No. 21 (University, Ala.: Alabama Museum of Natural History).

Struever, S., and K. D. Vickery, 1973. The Beginnings of Cultivation in the Midwest-Riverine Area of the United States. *American Anthropologist* 75 : 1197–1220.

Tainter, J., 1973. Social Correlates of Mortuary Patterning at Kaloko, North Kona, Hawaii. *Archaeology and Physical Anthropology in Oceania* 8 : 1–11.

————, 1975. *The Archaeological Study of Social Change: Woodland Systems in West-Central Illinois* (Ph.D. diss., Northwestern University).

White, D., G. Murdock, and R. Scaglion, 1971. Natchez Class and Rank Reconsidered. *Ethnology* 10 : 396–398.

Biocultural Adaptation in Prehistoric America: An Anthropological Biologist's Perspective

ELIOT D. CHAPPLE

I SHOULD make clear as a necessary beginning of this appraisal that the term I have chosen for my own labeling, that of *anthropological biology*, is by no means a mere play on words, some kind of substitute for biological or physical anthropology. It refers, rather, to the general biology of individual human beings in the exact science sense. It comprises the biochemical, physiological and, of course, genetic properties controlling the system characteristics of the organism. Because the fundamental dimensions of culture can be isolated and shown to be dependent on the species-specific biological inputs that facilitate habituations (or learning processes), they provide us with a set of constraints on the adaptations or adjustments of the individuals to each other and to the environmental situations controlling them, whether natural or of human creation. Since these constraints can be given dimensional form, they can be treated quantitatively together with the deterministic rhythms of the individual as a biological system (Chapple 1970 and 1971).

It is worth pointing out that biologists per se, in departments of biology and in the textbooks they write, rarely include the human species as part of the animal kingdom—that class of phenomena they study. *Homo sapiens* is dragged in by the heels, so to speak—I am tempted to say by the cranium—at the end of the book or course, superficially treated, and, at least, implicitly regarded as *too, too* different from other animals. In medical biology, research is overly concerned with aiding the development of the art of practice. There is a remarkable hiatus between medical and biological research, with the exception of a few limited areas.

In anthropology generally (excluding physical anthropology) and in the other behavioral sciences, the "animal" is left out. All attention is paid to the logical elaboration of isolable cultural configurations—technology, language, economics, the arts, and so on—which assumes the cerebral cortex to be primary in understanding humans and their ways, whereas the contrary is the case. The Spanish philosopher, Ortega y

Gasset, in a variety of writings—particularly his *Man and People* (1957)
—stresses the fact that *Homo sapiens* is a misnomer; rather, the species
should have been called *Homo insciens*, that is, stupid, ignorant, un-
knowing. The philosopher made clear that, as all experience teaches us,
it is very rare for human beings to manage moments of being *sapiens*.
Each of us is a creature of our emotional reactions, neuroendocrine and
physiological, able to short-circuit the cerebral cortex in the flash of a
moment of stress.

Anthropological biology is thus cross-species, cross-cultural, and, of
course, cross-historical. It finds no justification for the popular stereo-
type that only the human species has culture, nor can it substantiate the
fondly held belief that the neocortex enables *Homo sapiens* to transcend
the overpowering influences of the lower centers. It regards the *tabula
rasa* dogma of the Skinnerian and other types of psychologists, which
permeates too much of the behavioral sciences, as ridiculous in the face
of the evidence.

Anthropological biology, therefore, assigns a major role to physiological or behavioral genetics in contributing to the potentials of individuals,
in particular in emphasizing the endogenous properties of the biological
rhythms, the engines that drive us. These rhythms range from the very
fast frequencies of muscle fiber discharge—the heart, respiration, interaction—to the slower ones of the intradian bursts of interaction and activity, next and best studied to the circadian. Then, they include longer
cycles, like the oestrous cycle, up to the circannual, and perhaps beyond.
Anthropological biology recognizes the hard fact that the expression of
the gene can be inhibited, modified, or facilitated by environmental
influences.

More important, it regards population genetics as of little significance
in helping us to understand the system properties of individual organisms, for reasons that need not delay us (Chapple 1976). It emphasizes
the broad findings that the expressive characters of the gene are determined by the properties of regulatory genes (the operon). Through this
complex of regulatory genes, the rates and timing of onset of expression
are managed, rather than through the structural genes, traditionally relied on by many researchers, yet of little value in differentiating the developmental process that led to the profound morphological differences
between the human and the chimpanzee.

As a final comment on the discipline of anthropological biology, since
it is concerned with the dynamic process of individual living human beings (note my reiteration of "individual"), preoccupation with evolution
and population genetics as the be-all and end-all of biological theory is

clearly unnecessary. Extrapolation into the past may be an interesting exercise in detective work, but even to be able to do so depends on the degree to which we understand the process controlling the system properties of the living individual. This may place anthropological biology outside the mainstream of present-day fashion, but it makes possible a quantitative and exact formulation of what goes on without having to postulate, for the sake of a logical position adopted, the intervention of variables that are too fuzzy for scientific definition.

The primary concern of the papers presented in this volume is to make clear the increasing utility of precise examinations of skeletal materials and the environmental evidence at any given site. Most useful is the concern with exploring trace elements systematically, using the newest techniques as they appear, and relating this analysis to known biochemical and physiological properties characterizing the various states of health of individuals. This enables the biological or physical anthropologist to achieve a reliable estimate of important factors affecting the lives of individuals reflected in the skeletal materials excavated, to test their validity against other populations and against living material. I would hope that this would be done more extensively. With the increasing availability of highly sophisticated techniques of microanalysis in physics and biochemistry, a remarkable expansion in what can be included in such histories is becoming possible. Moreover, similar procedures can be utilized for soil analysis, the differential distribution of trace elements in the skeleton and particularly in the teeth, and the degree to which leaching, replacement, or unequal cumulation rates within any given soil chemical complex have to be taken into account.

It is clear, therefore, that the impact of diet, the level of nutritional balance, individual (idiosyncratic) variations in the developmental (maturation) process as well as the occurrence and severity of pathologies are now capable of being described with reasonable confidence. Evidence of types of mechanical wear operating on the teeth, supplemented by botanical and zoological data on the probable availability and utilization of varying types of food at a given time, leads to educated guesses as to historical change, for example, in the health of a given population.

A great many possibilities for further inquiry are tossed out passim along with the authors' concern with the major themes of their individual papers. Examples of these possibilities include the following: the equivalent musculature of males and females in the Annis shellmound, obscuring polymorphism; the nature of the nutritional disease that so uniformly affected the people at the Buckner site (disproportionate dependence on maize can bring about "tropical" sprue); the implications of magnesium deficiency for particular types of disorders of the central nervous system, which could create very marked pathologies in the relationships (interactions) of individuals.

With such specific points I have little disagreement; it is when we turn to the broader implications of these studies that I encounter difficulties. These can be classified under three headings: (*a*) inferences as to cultural (organizational) structuring; (*b*) the appropriateness of the statistical techniques used analytically; and (*c*) genetics. It is not that workers in this field are to be singled out invidiously. Rather, imprecision in utilizing inferences for establishing states of biocultural adaptation is endemic in a wide number of fields. This imprecision reflects either a lack of acquaintance with cross-cultural studies throughout the world or insufficient understanding of the limiting constraints of the assumptions that need to be satisfied in genetics, and in statistics, before these disciplines can be utilized to create explanatory hypotheses.

Consider the cultural (biocultural) deductions in these papers. If we assume, as we must, that we can only extrapolate to past situations—in this case made up of osteological and spatial distance-technological data from reasonably detailed descriptions of present-day or in any case even recent societies—then we have to ask whether alternative hypotheses cannot be brought up by way of contradiction. It became entirely clear to me on reading these papers, and no doubt is clear to the investigators themselves, that they have been strongly influenced by accounts of the earliest writers on American Indian societies in the midwestern and southern regions of the United States, and are familiar with the various attempts to reconstruct the cultures characterizing them.

This approach is perfectly natural as a point of departure. Necessarily, however, it requires us to assume that Hopewell, Fort Ancient, and other postulated cultures represented some kind of continuity to the ethnographic present—more complex perhaps, as evidenced in their mound construction, but relatively homologous just the same. Generalizations in regard to hierarchical differentiation provide no rebuttal to the criticisms that a Hindu anthropologist might make as he or she referred, for example, to the towering structures of tabus affecting diet and nutrition which are incorporated within what is superficially called the caste system. Whereas the present authors argue that dietary sufficiency would occur maximally in the highest rank of the postulated hierarchical order, our Hindu opponent would maintain the contrary argument by pointing out that the best diets, and by far the greatest physical development, are to be found in some, but by no means all, outcaste groups.

In the same way, take the much-discussed question as to the evidence for chiefdoms, social classes, or, more ambiguously, social stratification

and social status. When one asks what the criteria are for such differen-
tiations, the answer comes from a necessary reliance solely on the layout
of the burial plots, the amount, type and derivation of cultural objects,
and the distribution of types of individuals within the plot. Mortuary
elaboration in many cultures is associated with wealth and differential
position in the hierarchy, to whatever degree it exists or is elaborated.
Yet there is a remarkably large number of exceptions. These consist not
merely of those controlled by religious associations or institutions, but
those where for a variety of reasons objects are passed down to the sur-
vivors, with only a few spared for burials, or where destruction of the
objects and bodies in mortuary flames eliminates evidence for the osteologist.

Moosman (1976), in a study of a modern burial ground in Tucson,
Arizona, pointed out that low-income Mexican-Americans were characterized by differences in expenditures which appeared to be strongly
influenced by factors bringing about the death. Deaths due to drug over-
doses had minimal funerals and cultural objects; whereas, young women,
from even the poorest families, who had died of breast cancer were the
focus for great expenditures, aided by gifts from extended kin.

I am not saying that variants such as these—and others that could be
cited with appropriate references—necessarily hold in the case of the
prehistoric peoples under consideration. Yet, I believe that we have to
utilize the most rigorous criteria possible without automatically attributing social organizational characteristics to the material obtained through
the excavations. The scientific investigator must first be able to say with
reasonable confidence that certain uniformities are the only ones that
can be established. These conclusions must not be confounded by interpretative assumptions as to the cultural universe which on other grounds,
ordinarily historical, is believed to have been present. These cautions,
of course, apply equally to both archeologists and biological anthropologists.

After completing the above steps, we can begin to make inferences or
hypotheses explicitly. We can then say, "knowing these facts, and making the assumption that these people had these particular cultural con-
tinuities with recent people, so and so *might* be the case." In order to do
this, however, we must take one more step. We must ask ourselves
whether we have systematically examined, archeologically, the scope of
the culture—that is, can we satisfy ourselves that no alternate possibilities are tenable? This leads us to a crucial problem, the appropriateness
of the statistical treatments used. By what assumptions are we justified
in selecting them?

Although the use of statistics is commonly regarded as essential, perhaps conferring on the results a degree of sanctity that otherwise they would not attain, it is helpful to ask whether any particular statistical technique that appeals to the investigator or to an editor has any real legitimacy or adds anything to the information provided in tabulations of the primary data. I say this because throughout these articles two sets of assumptions have been added to justify statistical manipulation of the raw data of the skeletal and material culture remains and their spatial, as well as stratigraphic, relationships. These assumptions derive from demography and genetics and, in several articles, are explicitly used to construct complex hypotheses presumably validated by the statistics.

I believe that it is fundamental as a first principle in scientific work to make a clear differentiation between the raw data resulting from excavation, what the investigators actually find, and the hypothesis-building influences which can be derived by calling on demography and genetics. It is commonplace in statistics to emphasize that the place to begin is with the raw frequency distributions; only then can you determine how to proceed to choose a statistic. However commonplace, it is a rule that is usually ignored. Another problem is that when we talk of samples (for example, the actual yield of skeletal material worked up), these must be assumed to have been drawn from a homogeneous population. They can hence be treated as randomly selected, as the assumptions of the Gaussian equation require. It is quite obvious, however, from the analysis of the available skeletal material, apart from varying "sample" size, that many factors intervened to bias the selection process—state of preservation of the skeleton, "well-meant" cleaning of the bones, breakage, missing or badly preserved bones, lack of funds (or time or interest) for complete excavations of the site, and others.

It is also clear that the skeletal evidence does not yield a demonstrable approximation to any equation describing a specific frequency distribution—Gaussian, Poisson, binomial, exponential (and there are many others). Each of these requires certain assumptions to be fulfilled before they can be used. We gild the lily, then, if we use "tests of significance," etc., rather than comparing the distributions themselves. With data such as these, none of the assumptions, primarily Gaussian, are satisfied that are necessary for their use. We should remember that R. A. Fisher said in what may seem to some an overly simple approach that the greatest impediments to scientific advance are universities, to which I would add editors of scientific journals, their referees, and reviewers, all of whom insist on the blind use of cookbook statistics.

Nor am I impressed by Oxnard's (1974) attempt to rationalize the use of statistics derived from Gaussian distributions by saying that "although the blind approach to such techniques should be rightly abhorred, a response seems to be arising that *denigrates* (my emphasis) the applications because they are not . . . used *perfectly*. . . . Although one axiom of such methods is that data distributions be normal, and the careful worker attempts to test for this where possible, . . . non-normality of biological data does not upset the methods *to any great degree* (my emphasis) as long as the non-normality is *not gross*" (Oxnard 1974 : 172–173). I could cite at length the horrendous consequences of a similar philosophy in biomedical research when life and death are often at stake. Perhaps it is enough to say that the use of the italicized phrases without specification of criteria for determining what is a nongross, non-normal distribution, is like telling the judge that the girl is "a little bit pregnant." The other "available" methods to which he refers (taxonomic, multivariate statistics, Fourier transforms as used, and non-metrical "statistical" techniques), moreover, are all necessarily built on the shifting sands of the Gaussian equation, however towering and cloud-capped is the resulting edifice (regarded as the product). It is hard to accept the first axiom of the computer systems analyst: "input garbage"; but there it is, in all its inelegant phrasing.

Some of the authors in elaborating their discussions have been tempted to utilize demographic theories to ballast their statistical discussions. It should be emphasized that life tables and mortality tables are built on particular populations, usually those of the United States or Western European countries (though these are hardly homogeneous). These can no more be extrapolated to Woodland times than can their hypotheses as to malnutrition levels. Even more irrelevant and devoid of reality are the constructs demographers use which require populations to be stable, that is, of infinite size, no net immigration or emigration, with fixed rates of fertility and mortality at each age. This does not mean that conclusions may not be drawn from an eyeball view of the raw distributions—for instance, Etowah Mound C versus the village population—but the use of demographic "theory" is merely a contaminant.

Throughout the discussions, moreover, there is a hankering for the introduction of genetics into the population analysis in spite of the fact that very little has been established with regard to genetic factors in the skeleton. In spite of these admitted areas of our ignorance, however, temptation has overcome some of the authors. This has led to complex statistical analyses based on presumptions about the properties of the genotype that are statistically, as well as genetically, invalid.

We should be grateful, I suppose, that no author utilized the ecto-plasmic techniques of factor analysis—a mathematical and scientific will-of-the-wisp. Though developed by R. A. Fisher and first exemplified by him in a comparison of skulls, the multiple discriminant function has built into it the assumption that we are dealing with Gaussian distributions. This assumption also applies to the types of cluster analysis used. There are, I should add, nonstatistical forms of cluster analysis that to a considerable extent obviate some of these difficulties, though they create others.

From the point of view of statistics, it is important to remember that (*a*) even though a certain classification produces a difference that is greater between the classes than between individuals within the classes, in terms of the variables used, and (*b*) this difference is "statistically significant," this does *not* prove that the difference is anything but a mathematical product. It does not necessarily have biological uniformities to substantiate it. Even if we think there might be a biological explanation, this is post hoc. The biological explanation is not capable of being substantiated except by experiment, which clearly we are in no position to do with skeletal remains.

I will now turn to some of the genetic assumptions. Obviously this is not the place for a disquisition on the innumerable difficulties which the use or misuse of statistics in genetics creates. Difficulties are particularly acute when facilitated by computer programs, which are rarely developed by biologists for biological purposes. It is even more important to recognize the limitations of the material available and to focus on what it states rather than using a series of "iffy" assumptions about genetics transformed into statistics, which are admittedly not applicable. I find it difficult to see why some of the authors should talk either about single genes or about polygenes as determinants of discrete phenotypic traits in the human skeleton, or about gene flow or genetic distance, when our knowledge of the genotype is primarily characterized by ignorance.

I would remind you that in highly sophisticated biochemical analyses of proteins and nucleic acids, now available due to recent advances in molecular biology, comparisons of proteins and DNA in humans and chimpanzees have demonstrated that the structural genes of these two species are as similar as those of sibling species of other organisms. As a recent review by King and A. C. Wilson (1975) demonstrates, the structural genes in the two species are, in fact, on the average more than 99 percent identical. If structural genes cannot distinguish the profound morphological differences of the two species, how can we expect to use structural genes to determine differences between one excavated collection of Woodland skeletons and another? I am talking about genetics, remember, not anatomy.

Present evidence from physiological (and behavioral) genetics suggests that morphological, physiological, and ecology-adaptive differences are probably brought about by the regulatory genes. It is these which control the expression of the mutations of the genes through shifts in timing of activation or level of activity of single genes, probably in embryonic development. This does not mean that we cannot compare frequency distributions of the phenotypic expressions of structural genes as we can do in living material. However, to make a rabbit stew, you first have to catch your rabbit. This means that a great deal of experimental work is necessary in order to demonstrate their isomorphic properties in the various forms of skeletal expression we encounter in excavations. I do not think that quantitative physiological genetics is a particularly good candidate for model building, because the genetics of regulatory systems is not amenable to classical genetic strategies (Fuller 1964).

In summary, I do not want to leave the impression that I think that little can be hypothecated from the analysis of skeletal, environmental, and material culture findings by physical anthropologists and archeologists, who are using the data obtained through excavations. The above strictures are from the point of view of an anthropological biologist who must also be an applied mathematician and statistician. What I am saying is that the shoemaker should stick to his last. Hence, I urge biological anthropologists and archeologists to limit themselves to the materials they obtain and to use the simplest and most explicit assumptions with which to generalize. Remember that once you have identified the uniformities in such a way that no one can argue with them, you can proceed to feel free to suggest alternate hypotheses as to cultural implications of the uniformities you have established. If you accept as a first premise the likelihood of a continuity backward in time—say from the Muskogean people, particularly the Creeks, or elsewhere by a different course from the Shawnee—then say so. Make clear that you are restricting the hypothesis-forming process to what might be applicable to early forms of such a culture. At the same time, be sure your readers understand that you are not making statements that you think should hold across cultures, as the statements clearly do not do.

I think you should be equally cautious, moreover, in making assumptions about social organization. That there are differences in burial spacing and topographic relationships and differences in the presence or absence of particular types of artifacts (for example, Hopewell) establishes that there were differences between individuals in utilizing these criteria. What these "mean" is a different question. Among other things, it does *not* mean that rank, social classes, "ascribed" or "achieved" status, the division of labor, and so on are demonstrable or improbable, except by dint of extrapolation.

I cannot take the time to treat these fashionable categories of social structure in terms of the ambiguities in definition they present in the literature or to outline the criteria that are necessary if they are to be defined rigorously. If the logical first step is to postulate a culture, the Creeks, for instance, as the modern-time cultural descendants of the Woodland peoples, then projections backward in time require the criteria to be worked out for the Muskogean people first. This, of course, is not your immediate concern; but it means that, in addition to including the archeologists and other specialists necessary for your work, biological anthropologists need to urge the sociocultural anthropologists or ethnologists to provide you with a reasonably firm ground to develop alternate hypotheses restricted to the actual data you describe.

I would, in fact, strongly support and give even greater emphasis to the point made in several of the papers that biological or physical anthropologists should be much more demanding of their archeological colleagues. They should demand microexcavation methods of recovery of all essential data to answer the many questions whose importance has been described so well in these papers. This is particularly true when one considers the potential contributions of trace element analysis. In addition, the complexities and difficulties of sampling should also make it imperative for the archeologists to conduct their excavations more systematically, not simply within the stratigraphic sequence, but across what might be called the land-use environment of the population to its boundaries. I recognize that this takes time and money. Sampling theory, however, can be more properly worked out for a land area and applied to actual excavation procedures after exploratory surveys have been completed than it can be worked out for and applied to erratically obtained and insufficient skeletal and environmental data. It is the latter with which the physical anthropologists have so far had to contend.

REFERENCES

Chapple, E. D., 1970. *Culture and Biological Man: Explorations in Behavioral Anthropology* (New York: Holt, Rinehart, and Winston).
———, 1971. Toward a Mathematical Model of Interaction: Some Preliminary Considerations. In *Explorations in Mathematical Anthropology*, P. Kay, ed. (Cambridge: MIT Press), pp. 141–178.
———, 1976. The Emperor Has No Clothes! Review of *Sociobiology: The New Synthesis*, by E. O. Wilson (Cambridge: Belknap Press of Harvard University Press). *Reviews in Anthropology* 3: 109–114.
Fuller, J. L., 1964. Physiological and Population Aspects of Behavior Genetics. *American Zoologist* 4: 101–109.
King, M-C., and A. C. Wilson, 1975. Evolution at Two Levels in Humans and Chimpanzees. *Science* 188:107–116.

Moosman, J. E., 1976. Ethnographic Funerals and Archeological Burials: The View from the Mortuary. (Manuscript on file, Arizona State Museum, University of Arizona.)

Ortega y Gasset, 1957. *Man and People*, W. R. Trask, tr. (New York: W. W. Norton).

Oxnard, C. E., 1974. A Note on Quantification and Analysis. In *Yearbook of Physical Anthropology*, J. Buettner-Janusch, ed. (Washington, D.C.: American Association of Physical Anthropologists), pp. 172–173.

The Contributors

ROBERT L. BLAKELY is Assistant Professor of Anthropology at Georgia State University. His B.A. and PH.D. degrees in physical anthropology are from Indiana University with minor fields in archeology, anatomy, zoology, and psychology. Research interests include the somatometric study of living nonhuman primates and the laboratory and computer analyses of Amerindian skeletons.

JANE ELLEN BUIKSTRA is Associate Professor of Anthropology at Northwestern University. She received the M.A. and PH.D. degrees from the University of Chicago and has done research in archeology focusing on eastern woodlands populations. Her interest is in the study of prehistoric skeletal populations emphasizing microevolutionary change and biological response to environmental stress, using a multidisciplinary approach.

ELIOT D. CHAPPLE is currently affiliated with the Medical Engineering Laboratory, Stevens Institute of Technology, Hoboken, New Jersey. He earned both B.A. and PH.D. in anthropology from Harvard University and has specialized in anthropological biology, with psychiatry as a secondary applied field. His most recent book, *Culture and Biological Man*, is a statement of the ways in which he sees the human condition being effectively described within the framework of biology.

ROBERT I. GILBERT, JR., is Assistant Professor of Anthropology at the University of Southern Mississippi, having received his M.A. from the University of Alabama and his PH.D. from the University of Massachusetts. In addition to his study of trace elements, his research interests include cultural change and social biology, nutrition and disease patterns, and osteological development and degeneration.

CHRISTOPHER S. PEEBLES is associated with the Museum of Anthropology, University of Michigan, Ann Arbor. He received M.A. and PH.D. degrees from the University of California, Santa Barbara, and has done extensive research on prehistoric southeastern cultures. He is currently the Associate Editor of *American Antiquity*.

ANTHONY JAMES PERZIGIAN is Associate Professor of Anthropology at the University of Cincinnati. He received the PH.D. in anthropology from Indiana University and has done postdoctoral work in human genetics and societal problems, sponsored by the National Science Foundation. His research interests include physical anthropology, evolution, human variation and adaptation, osteology, and dental anthropology.

LOUISE M. ROBBINS is Associate Professor of Anthropology, University of North Carolina, Greensboro. Her M.A. and PH.D. were received at Indiana University with special emphasis on the prehistoric Shawnee people. She is interested in the effects of diverse environmental, nutritional, and cultural factors on the form and functioning of human populations through time.

DAVID J. WOLF is Assistant Professor of Anthropology at the University of Kentucky. His degrees are from University of North Carolina, M.A. in archaeology, and University of Arizona, PH.D. in physical anthropology. Research interests include human genetics and microevolution, osteology, and demography. He has studied prehistoric populations of the southeastern United States, Mesoamerica, and highland South America, and has also studied nonhuman primate species.